AF812825

Making More Money for YOU!™

Wealth Building Through Indexed Universal Life Investments

By Magnus Carter

Table of Contents

Introduction

Adult life is tough, but I can guide you to make it much easier. Whether you are 25 or 50 years old, you need to keep making money to survive. Bills, rent, groceries, tuition loans, all these responsibilities get thrown at us after we start living by ourselves without much warning. It becomes tiring and stressful after a while, but we keep going. We continue to work, waiting for our sweet retirement. Unfortunately, the bitter truth is that most of us will not have enough money to retire in the future.

Right now, you may be energized enough to pull all-nighters and do three jobs at once, but that is an unrealistic way of life. Soon, old age will catch up, and you will be forced to work at the same pace. That is not possible.

What if there was a way to grow wealth without breaking one's back all the time? Does money have to be this hard and tiresome to get? Is there anything you can do to change your future and see your children and grandchildren go to college without worrying? A sure-fire solution to all your financial problems can be acquired easily by diving into the money-making industry of investing.

Sure, some people will be fine letting their money sit in the bank account for all their life, but no bank account in the world can save your money from losing its value with time. As we enter and experience the biggest inflation crisis of the century, you can see that prices have doubled since last year. You need to spend 2 dollars for an item worth 1 dollar in the past, which means the money reduced its purchasing power due to inflation. All the hard-earned savings people did have been cut in half. Luckily for investors, their money has not.

Investing is a tried and tested method of building wealth and has helped people escape poverty and made some into millionaires. However, investing comes with its risks, with a fair share of failure stories. The fear of failure keeps most people from getting into investing and not taking the opportunity to become financially independent.

If you are one of those people worried about the ups and downs of investment, there is a solution for you as well. There is a way to invest by minimizing risks and guaranteeing a profit at the end of the year, no matter if the stocks are not doing well. It is called Index Universal Life Investments.

To earn good money with stocks, funds, and bonds, one needs to put a lot of effort and time into learning and then invest in the best choices by themselves, with risks of their choices ending up a dud. Index Universal Life Investments are different. To earn good money with it, you only need to pay an amount at specified periods, just like insurance, and you are done. The money will grow at a higher rate than inflation, basically securing your retirement and fire plans, whether it be buying a house, going on foreign trips, etc. You will reap all the benefits of investment without any hard work involved.

You may be wondering why you should listen to me. As any other teenager, I thought that everyone needed to work hard to make money, so I began working as soon as I was able to. When working at a diner in New York City, I came into contact with many successful men and women and tried my best to find the secret of their wealth. As a result of those conversations, my worldview shifted. For the first time, I understood that savings could be used as a money-making tool itself. Being young, I was still open to new ideas, which is why I am able to live comfortably now. Not only my present, but the future of my wife and kids will be secure. I am able to fulfill my responsibilities and my own desires, all because I got into investing at an early age.

Since I was able to, I began to educate others about different financial options and choices and help them get to the point of life where they want to be. First, it started with friends, family, and colleagues. The information they learned turned out to be useful enough that they kept coming for more and more. The gap in financial knowledge among people was becoming more obvious. Later on, I dedicated myself to giving financial education to others and providing an option for anyone struggling to turn their life around.

Upon giving advice, I noticed some people would hesitate to take action and follow the routine as usual. Taking the advice would solve all their problems. Later I found that the fear of losing hard-earned money was too great of an emotion for people to take such risks.

It is completely understandable for someone to be worried about their money; it is a lifeline. Moreover, keeping track of your stocks and the value of your assets is a difficult task. Many people barely have time to rest from their everyday lives, so investing is not a good choice. But because money is so important that you and I need to take financial options seriously. Perhaps opting for the IUL investment is the step you need to achieve your dreams finally. You will only know if you learn about it.

There are a lot of financial plans out there which grow your money for retirement. 401k, having a savings account, and getting bonds are a few of them. However, you have to decide what plan is right for you carefully, what plan suits your goals, and most importantly, what plan is the most profitable for your situation. You will learn about all the types of investment options out there, how you can choose the perfect one, what exactly is Index Universal Life Investments are , and how they might answer your needs.

Learning to improve on your retirement life is a big step you have already taken. You will be able to work carefree and sleep soundly at night, knowing that you have picked the best option for the future. Not only you, but your family will benefit and live a happy life because of your decisions. So, keep reading and unlock many more pieces of advice and tips to improve your life.

There will be many who talk about taking action, but unfortunately, very few will follow through on their goals. It is great that you have started to learn and think about retirement, but know that if you just read and do not implement any techniques in the real world, you will gain any benefit from this book.

To start working on your future endeavors, you must first know what Index Universal Life Investments is.

Chapter 1: Where Did IUL Come From?

It is sad to know that many people make their lifelong financial decisions with incomplete information. You will only hear about a plan if it is constantly advertised on TV or social media, such as life insurance, etc. There are many more options out there, and remaining ignorant of them might become why you never find a suitable retirement plan in the present or future. Even if you consider IUL to not be your cup of tea, it is important that you make this choice mindfully and with all the pros and cons laid out. That being said, first, you have to understand what IUL or Indexed Universal Life Investments is.

What is Indexed Universal Life Investments/Insurance?

Indexed Universal Life Investments/Insurance can be seen as permanent life insurance. This means that primarily the program builds up wealth over the years, decades even, and releases an amount when you pass away.

Fact: A plan that releases some amount of funds upon the death of the plan owner is called giving a "death benefit."

This insurance plan is not unique and is a part of other whole-life policies anyone is open to apply. Examples of other whole-life policies are:

- Universal Life Insurance
- Variable Universal Life Insurance

(IUL) can be written as both Indexed Universal Life Insurance and Indexed Universal Life Investments because they are bought as an insurance-investment hybrid policy and have the properties of both plans served in one.

Most of us have some idea about life insurance. However, most are still unaware of the entire buffet of types they come in. Life insurance can be:

- Fixed-rated or
- Variable

Fixed-rated means that they give you a fixed number of returns, while variable, as the name suggests, gives unequal amounts depending on the type of account you have decided to invest in.

Fact: Returns, in economics, is a term to describe a profit or how much money is given back to you.

Indexed Universal Life Investments are a type of life insurance that allows a person to place or put money towards fixed-rate or variable accounts. However, Indexed Universal Life Investments variable accounts only work with equity indexes.

What Are Indexes?

If you are new to investments and do not know anything about the stock market, then the term "indexes" might be new to new. An index is nothing more than a measuring tool that different industries use. In economics and investment, indexes show how well a big chunk of shares is doing in the stock market. They are used to figuring out price performances and answer basic questions. Are they doing well, and the value is high, or are they going down, and the value is low? Knowing whether the stock market is doing well or not helps in making future decisions regarding investments and even decides whether we want to keep investing or not.

Noting down the value of price performances or index values reveals how well the shares are performing over the years, giving additional information on whether to invest in a share. If the values are constantly going up and increasing, it means that the share is growing and bringing in more money by going up in price. On the other hand, if the value is constantly decreasing, it means that the share is shrinking and losing money by going down in price.

There are thousands of Indexes keeping records of the price performances of different industries, but the most popular ones are Nasdaq-100 or S&P-500. They give information about the price performances of major companies across multiple sectors.

Fact: Shares are a type of asset that shows a percentage of ownership in a company or cooperation. When a person buys a company's share, they buy a piece of that company and get profits accordingly.

IUL Insurance and Indexes

Indexed Universal Life Investments work with indexes to provide profit and build wealth over time. Traditionally, investment requires you to buy index stocks directly, which increase and decrease along with the price performances and the Indexes. With IUL investment, they do this process for you. An indexed universal life investment is less risky than directly buying stocks or getting a variable Universal Life insurance. However, it is riskier than fixed Universal Life Investments.

Fact: A fixed universal life insurance is the least risky, but the returns are also the lowest compared to other types. It is a general rule of thumb that if any asset, policy, or share has more money-making potential, it is usually riskier and has a higher chance of losing money as well.

IUL investment policies work as a retirement plan because they accumulate wealth over time until retirement, while being exempted from tax cuts. It will also provide a death benefit to your family members, similar to life insurance. You will receive the benefits of both policies and the opportunity to invest in the stock market with fewer risks and a higher chance of getting more returns.

IUL investments are not common and are considered advanced life insurance policies because they have more technical details and are more complicated than other plans. Fortunately, once you understand it, they can prove to be useful. If you are someone that needs a permanent life insurance policy but also wants to invest in the stock market can use this method to do both at the same time. Normally you have to pay a life insurance policy and put money in a stock market account separately. Still, you can do both with just one type of payment. Business owners, people looking to work in real estate, and people with finance backgrounds all prefer IUL investment as a serious option for their financial planning.

How Does an IUL Investment Work?

Now that we know what IUL investments are, we must understand how they function. It is necessary that anyone seriously considering this option has an idea about the inner workings of this policy so they can be fully aware of how their money is being used.

When a person purchases an IUL investment policy, they become a policyholder. As a policyholder, the person needs to pay a premium payment to maintain the policy, just like a life insurance plan. However, just one part of the payment covers the life insurance aspect. The payment is unevenly distributed to contribute to other aspects as well. These are:

- Growing overall cash value
- Costs of administrative and premium expenses
- Costs or commissions and fees

Cash value is an important part of IUL investment. The insurance company ties the cash that has been paid to a market index, such as the S&P 500 or any other index of their choice.

It is the insurance company that decides what index your money is going to be tied up with or following the growth. Technically, the money is not being 'invested.' If it was invested, then there is a chance your money could be lost. Instead, the insurance company decides which index's growth will determine your wealth's growth. For example, suppose the market is doing exceptionally well, and there has been an increase of 10%. In that case, your account value, corresponding with this growth, will also increase by 10%. However, the major downside is that the growth has a cap rate. It can only grow till that cap rate, and no further. If the cap rate is around 12%, then even if the market has gone up 15-20%, you will only receive 12% returns.

Fact: The cap rate can be described as an upper limit on how much your equity/funds can grow with the policy. The growth cannot be higher than the limit specified. The cap is usually rated around 10-12% with Indexed Universal Life Investments.

This happens when there is positive growth in the market. Perhaps you might wonder what happens if the market value tanks or goes down at a loss. In this case, fortunately, the insurance company does not lower your wealth in the policy. There is, typically, a lower guaranteed growth limit with IUL investments. It is one of the biggest advantages of this policy. This limit, however, is variable and changes with different insurance providers. So, this investment plan has almost no chance of losing money.

Indexed Universal Life Investments policies last for the policyholder's entire life as long as the premiums are paid on time. As time passes and the policyholder gets older, the premium costs increase. However, this increase in payment can be lowered or adjusted accordingly by lowering the death benefit. This means your family will get less money when you die, but the premium costs will be manageable for you, and other benefits the policy provides will also be active.

A policyholder cannot take any money out of the policy until sufficient cash has been built up. After this amount has been built, you can take money out, but you must pay the amount back with interest. Failing to do so will cause a deduction from the death benefit.

You may be wondering whether the same laws apply to stocks and shares also apply to this investment. In 2010, the Dodd-Frank Wall Street Reform and Consumer Protection Act was passed, making IUL exempt from federal regulations. This means that the Department of the U.S. Securities and Exchange Commission does not oversee these investment policies. This is different from stocks and other options because the department regulates them. There is also less of a requirement needed to qualify to be an IUL stockbroker, meaning they might not give the best advice to you. Although, you can ask for financial advice from other stockbrokers instead and only consult these IUL brokers for only IUL investment information.

In short…

When you decide to follow an IUL investment/insurance policy, you have to take it out with the help of an IUL stockbroker. The policy provider will determine the insurance company associated with the IUL investment policy. The insurance company can decide or help you decide what index to use to tie your policy account. The Index's growth will decide how much returns you get, meaning how much wealth will be built and be served as your death benefit. The insurance fees will be determined by the policyholder's age; the older, the higher. The premium you pay will be used to pay all the fees associated with the policy, and the remaining amount will be added to your account.

Fact: The money in your policy account will be referred to as cash value.

As years go by, the cash value will also increase with interest-based returns associated with the chosen index. After a specified cash value is reached, the policyholder can take out the money whenever they want. However, this is borrowed money and needs to be paid back with interest attached. In the case where the loan cannot be returned, or the policyholder does not wish to return, the same amount will be cut from the death benefit. No additional cuts will occur.

It is important to note that not every IUL investment policy is the same, and the benefits and drawbacks depend on what provider you have chosen and what index you can opt to follow. Commonly, IUL investment policies have a guaranteed minimum return, so keep your eye out for the best deal. Some policies may also give you the option of choosing a fixed indexed account, meaning the amount increasing will be at the same rate no matter how much the market value has increased or decreased.

The percentage of return will be determined by monthly index price performance. The value at the beginning of the month will be compared to that at the end of the month, and the increase or decrease in the Index will determine how much money is added to your cash value.

Example of IUL Investment

To further familiarize ourselves and remove any mistakes in our understanding, let's look at an example concerning IUL investment.

Consider an index fund that has increased 5% in value from the 1st of March till the 31st of March. Now, because there is a 5% increase, the cash value in our policy's account will be multiplied by 5%. The resultant value will be added as interest gains into the cash value.

Fact: Usually, the policy calculates index gains by comparing the price value of the Index for a certain period, but others can calculate it as average daily changes for a month as well.

The percentage rate the insurance company calculates to add to your policy account is called the "participation rate." This is the amount of index gain going to the life insurance company. It can be anywhere from 25 to 100% based on your policy account.

Fact: Index gains are the profit or money you get in your account from the index increase in value.

Let's say the index gain is around 6%, and the insurance company has set the participation rate as 50%. If your cash value is currently $10,000, then:

$$= .06 \times .50 \times 10{,}000$$

$$= \$300$$

The amount of $300 will then be added to the cash value. The index gains will be credited into your account once a year or every five years.

Are IUL Investment Policies Popular?

Although the concept of IUL investment is relatively new, these programs are being bought regularly and have been providing benefits for decades. The IUL investment policies are, first and foremost, life insurance policies being monitored by LIMRA, and their reports show a constant growth of this type of life insurance over the years.

Fact: LIMRA is short for "Insurance Marketing and Research Association." They primarily research life insurance policies for different companies.

Life insurance is being taken out more than ever; however, IUL investments showed the fastest growth than any other options of personal life insurance in 2021. It accounted for 20% of all the premiums paid that year. That is because IUL provides much more than a death benefit.

In surveys, IUL Policyholders say they wanted a clear life insurance policy and were also interested in growing their investment portfolio. With IUL providing them both with one payment, it satisfied both of their goals.

A properly structured and maintained policy account works as an efficient accumulating vehicle. To maintain a proper account, you will need to pay the maximum premium whenever possible and keep the death benefit to a minimum. Doing so will ensure that the policy expenses remain low and there are more premium payments you can give to grow your cash value.

IUL investment attracts more people because of the way the cash value increases. The interest is credited into the account by following the growth of the stock market indexes, which gives higher returns than other permanent life insurance policies. The returns are guaranteed after 1-5 years, according to the policy provider.

Moreover, even when the stock market crashes or goes down, the money will not be taken out of the account. It will never be negative, and in the worst cases, you will only have a 0% return. When dealing with the stock market, risks are part of the process. IUL's investment policy negates it completely.

For example

Consider a policyholder that has chosen to follow the S&P 500 index with a 10% cap. You paid your premium on 1st January when the Index was trading at 5000. Your policy provider will track the Index for a year till Dec 31st. The company will see how the Index is doing at this time. If the Index shows it is trading below our original value of 5000, then your cash value will not receive any interest, and it will be 0%. No matter how low, 4500, or 3000, your cash value will not lose money.

On the other hand, if the Index shows an increase of 11%, your account will only add 10% of the cash value because 10% is the cap limit.

Different policies also have different features attached to them. Finding one that suits a policyholder's individual needs is not difficult. It may be another reason people choose IUL over other policies.

History of IUL Investments: Where Did IUL Come From?

A Need for A New Life Insurance Policy

IUL investment may be a new method of life insurance policy, but its core concepts are already well-established ideas. The two parts of this insurance policy are permanent life insurance and fund accumulation through stocks, which were very popular financial systems. Many professionals working in finance and economics studied and researched both systems in quite a detail.

The idea of combining both was discussed by many during the middle of the 1900s. In 1971, Canadian President G.R. Dinney held an address to the Canadian Institute of Actuaries discussing the problems of life insurance companies. In his address, he warned the finance leaders at the time about the troubles in the insurance industry and proposed a solution called the "Universal Life Plan."

It was clear at the time that the social and economic stress was impacting all sectors of business, including life insurance. However, how they will impact them and the solutions are still unclear. Four years later, in 1975, the changes became even more apparent, and many people in the financial sector demanded practical solutions. At this time, C.H. Anderson, President of Tillinghast & Company, stepped up to further define the concept of a "Universal Life Insurance Policy." He made many speeches and articles, which made them more popular among his colleagues.

What Convinced Life Insurance Companies?

He said in his articles that social and economic instability made traditional life insurance weak and irrelevant compared to the market. At the time, the Canadian public was ill-informed and became extremely doubtful about life insurance policies. Inflation and increasing taxes made them rethink their entire financial plan, including insurance. With all the problems and the life insurance industry's inability to keep up with the rising prices, people started to leave traditional life insurance policies.

They started to look for programs that tied the life insurance policy and the good-performing market. This way, the policy could beat inflation. When all this happened, life insurance companies started to panic that they would lose all their customers at this rate. Because the economy was not doing well, the remaining policyholders took out more loans and had problems paying their premiums, which created cash flow problems in the industry. The problems made companies make low-profit decisions and lose out on benefits. All of these problems were discussed in Anderson's articles.

Fact: Cash flow deals with how money enters and leaves an organization

To escape from this vicious cycle, he advises the life insurance companies to use these social and economic changes to their advantage and bring ideas to the table. With married women working side by their husbands, the average household income increased. More and more families were able to pay for securities; in a sense, the number of potential customers increased for life insurance companies.

With increasing family income, more families started to qualify for higher tax brackets, where huge taxes were taken. Because life insurance policies gave a tax advantage, these families could appreciate life insurance policies more and see them more than death benefit providers.

The Main Idea Behind IUL

Mr. Anderson highly recommended "Universal Life Insurance Policy" as a solution to all these problems. He suggested a program that would allow the new higher-income families to not only get life insurance but also give them additional financial benefits while keeping the tax benefits as well. The new plan would also have a more flexible way of paying premiums. Flexible payment means that people will have full control over how long and when they want to pay for the insurance.

These ideas made the policies look more attractive to the people and made them want to try their policies. Also, they allowed people to participate in the stock market and get a chance to get a higher interest return than any traditional life insurance policy could give.

A Successful Launch

The financial heads saw potential in this plan, so they decided to test it out. Mr. Anderson, to describe in detail how his ideas would work, created a hypothesis. He described a life insurance company called "Cannibal Life." This life insurance company's name was used in the media and was heavily advertised to the public. The entire insurance industry and activity consumer groups also supported it. Soon it was seen that hundreds of thousands of people began to change their policies into Universal Life Policies. It was a huge success.

Seeing how well the Universal Life Policies did, other insurance companies started their own universal life insurance programs. In a few years, they secured a big portion of the market.

As new companies started to get into Universal Life Policies, they made subtle changes with time. They helped increase the commission rates, which led to the restructuring of the distribution system, making the entire process more efficient. This also reduced the costs of premiums that the investor needed to pay. More families could join this plan with reduced costs, and insurance companies' consumers significantly increased. Now, permanent whole life insurance plans have become even more separate than these policies.

In the end, all the companies either offered Universal Life Insurance or had some connection to the market. The insurance industry was changed completely, and the market, which was close to death, increased its worth to record-high levels.

Solidifying Universal Life Insurance

While Universal Life Insurance did well over the years, it did not perform as well during the early attempts. The early policies were very different and did not get as much attention. A Universal Life Insurance Policy was issued in 1977. It was marketed as a term life insurance policy and a deferred annuity.

Fact: Deferred annuity is the payment given to the policyholder after a certain period of time from the insurance company.

This system does not work because the payment given by the insurance as deferred annuity became a tax problem for policyholders. The campaign may also have failed because it was not as aggressively advertised or supported by other groups.

In 1979, the First Capital Life insurance company issued its own version of Universal Life Insurance. They combined the elements into a single contract, and the program was called Complete Life. This was more successful than its predecessor, and many companies started to copy their models for themselves. This phase happened in 1980-82 with new companies joining in continually, some major ones and some small. By the start of 1984, Universal Life Policies were being issued by almost every insurance provider with plenty of versions of them. The issue regarding taxes and tax cuts was also made clear in this phase when the passage of tax acts of 1982 and 1984 was passed. They were important in removing doubts and uncertainty behind Universal Life Insurance Policies, and they became an established product. These policies' future was bright and is now open to be discussed as any other securities. More features and versions were made and updated accordingly. This improvement movement gave birth to Indexed Universal Life Investments in the later years.

What are Indexed Universal Life Investments Annual Resets?

We have discussed how IUL works, but a common feature that makes it even more different from other life insurance policies is the annual reset. To completely understand IUL investments, you need to know what annual resets are.

Annual reset is a feature of IUL that guarantees that the policyholder's money is not lost. It ensures that every year's interest amount or returns are locked till the end of the year, and a new starting point is determined from the next day. Once a year's worth of returns enters your account, the money cannot be taken back due to bad market performance. When the term is going, market fluctuation will affect your return. The money invested will grow, but after a certain point, it will become a guarantee after the term has ended; the market has no effect on your cash value.

In this way, the money will continue to build up as you get the advantages of compounding interest from the Index, but you will not see a negative performance or money leaving out of your account once it goes in. Money will only increase and not decrease.

For example

Assume that you paid a premium on a policy on Jan 1st with the stock market functioning at 3500. Now, with a one-year term, that Index is trading at 3000 on Dec 31st. The end value of the Index is 500 points lower than when the premium was bought on Jan 1st. If you bought regular stocks, you would expect a loss of 10% from your principal investment. Fortunately, in IUL, you will not lose any money even though the index rating is down 500 points.

Fact: Principal investment is the initial money you have put into your account.

This is the result of an annual reset in IUL investments. You will be saved from any losses due to the risk involving the market, and you will not need to worry about losing your life insurance policy either. It is a safe way to add more investment assets. After the year ends on Dec 31st, the new value if Index is recorded for the next term on Jan 1st of the next year. Any gains during this period will be calculated and added to your account.

Besides giving a life insurance plan and investment gains, a person also has peace of mind. Setbacks involving finance can shake a person's entire life, and to save for the future efficiently and your family without worry is no less than a blessing. You will also keep on growing your assets without any negative performance. The key factor that made these policies popular is this annual reset feature giving protection to policyholders

How Do IUL Caps Work?

The gains or returns you will receive at the end of your term will be determined by the policy program you have chosen. You can choose common indexes with which to tie your policy account, like Dow Jones, NASDAQ, and S&P 500. Caps on these indexes are around 9-12%.

Fact: Remember that the policies have some changes in their terms, features, and caps, so you must choose a plan after a great deal of research.

These caps were not always at this level. Just 5 years ago, companies were giving policies with a 15% cap range. Sadly, they have decreased over time. One reason for lowering them is that the cost of getting the money tied to the Index had increased. In other words, internal fees have increased, and companies have compensated for it through lower caps.

Returning to indexes, there are more plentiful indexes to choose from than the most common ones. New policy providers offer new indexes to join all the time insurance companies. If you choose an index that is not as popular, you might be able to get higher caps on your policy and better returns over the years. These new indexes also help companies by cutting their expenses.

Some new indexes that are becoming popular choices are:

- Fidelity Multifactor Yield Index.
- Bloomberg U.S. Dynamic Balance II ER Index.
- PIMCO ER Index, etc.

These indexes come with higher cap limits; some even offer you policies with no caps. That is because these companies manage the not-so-popular indexes in-house and have full control over the decision-making processes of stock selection.

You can even follow more than one index at a time. Consider a scenario in which you have decided to participate in both Bloomberg and PIMCO indexes. You might be able to find a plan with no cap limit and a 140% participation rate. If the stocks grow in any one of them, let's say, 10%, you will see a gain of 14%. The participation rate increases the returns as well.

How Does a Person Take Money Out of Their Account?

Anyone can take money out of their cash value through withdrawals and loans.

Withdrawals

If a person makes a withdrawal from their account, the cash value is decreased permanently, and the reduced amount will be used for investing. Because it is a life insurance policy, the withdrawals will be free from income tax according to how much premium you have paid. There may be additional charges with withdrawals as well.

Loans

Taking loans is the main way a person accesses their cash value from an IUL account. The term loan may scare you, but these loans will not significantly harm you even if you do not pay them. If, at any point in your life, you want to withdraw, let's say, take a home equity loan to buy a house, you can use your cash value from the account instead. A great fact about them is that it is tax excepted as well.

You opt for two types of loans when taking money out of the account. They are:

- Standard loans
- Variable loans

Among the two, variable loans are much more common, which will be discussed later on.

Summary

- IUL investment/insurance is a type of insurance policy that grows in value with the market.
- There are many Universal Life Insurance Policies, and IUL is one of them.
- Indexes measure how a specific portion of the stock market shares is performing.
- The returns in a policyholder's IUL account are directly proportional to the growth of the Index that the person has chosen.
- There are two types of IUL investment policies, variable and fixed.
- Variable policies are riskier than fixed policies.
- IUL investment/insurance is taken out when a person pays the premiums defined by the policy.
- The premiums are used to pay administrative fees and commission fees. The rest is added to the account to increase its cash value.
- Cash value is the total amount of money you have in your account and will be used to invest in indexes.
- The Index will increase your cash value as it grows in its points for the period allotted to a certain level. This level determines the maximum profit you can receive and is known as Cap Limit or Cap Rate.
- IUL policies usually guarantee a lower limit guarantee and prevent money from decreasing, even if the index decreases in points.
- The policy is for life; however, premiums costs increase over the years. The end cash value will become your death benefit, which can be released to your family after your passing.

- Money can be taken out, but there will be cuts involved with it.
- IUl insurance/investment policies are tax exempted.
- IUl investment policies are getting more and more attention over the years.
- IUL investment policies history dates to the 1970s when the Canadian President and financial leaders noticed the insurance companies' downfall.
- After much speculation, economics experts came up with the idea that a life insurance policy should be linked with the market; thus, universal life investment/insurance was born.
- Annual Reset is the feature of IUL that prevents money from ever decreasing in the main account. This safeguard is why IUl is famous and considered to be a good option.
- There are two ways to take out money from your account: withdrawals or loans. Policies will have some withdrawal limits, after which you will need to take out a loan. Fortunately, you do not necessarily need to pay the loan back.

Chapter 2: Types of IUL's

Universal Life Investments/Insurance is further divided into different types to suit people with different backgrounds and unique goals. Because there are many options to choose from, more people find it suitable for their needs, and the popularity of this program has been increasing consistently. Universal Life Policies make up the majority of premium market shares, according to LIMRA. Among all of them, Index and Fixed types take up about 34% or one-third of all life insurance premiums. The second most popular is variable life insurance policies, taking up 13%. These are the most prominent among the many we are going to discuss.

Fact: LIMRA is an organization that researches and releases its findings on insurance companies and their products. LIMRA stands for "Life Insurance and Market Research Association."

Guaranteed Universal Life Insurance

Guaranteed universal life investment/insurance, or GUL is a type of policy in which the premium payments do not change with time as the policyholder ages, as in the case of other types. The death benefit will also be the same and will not reduce.

In this policy, the premium payment is selected based on what age you have set the policy to end. One can select any age, such as 80 or 120, and the policy will end when the person reaches this age. Choosing this age is an important factor in guaranteed universal life insurance because the higher the age, the more expensive the premium will be.

It is extremely similar to a regular life insurance policy and generally has very little cash value, if any. However, it is the cheapest type of universal life insurance one can buy. Till the age you have set, you will need to complete the premium payments.

Another term for the guaranteed universal life insurance policy is "No Lapse Guarantee Universal Life Insurance." This term highlights the advantage this policy has: the payments will not change no matter the circumstances. In recent years, non-guarantee universal life insurance has lapsed because it could not cover all the expenses. Suddenly, by force, the holders of this non-guarantee insurance had to pay much more expensive premiums, which they had never signed up for.

Due to these incidents, no-lapse policies have their own attractiveness. However, the biggest problem is that you can never miss or be late with the premium payments. Otherwise, the policy might end right there and then. Unlike traditional Index Universal Life Insurance Policies, there is no cash value associated with this policy, and you will have no money to take away when the policy ends. All the premiums you paid until then are non-refundable, and the insurance company will keep them forever, leaving you empty-handed. It is safe to say this policy is not for everyone.

Who Can Benefit from Guaranteed Universal Life Insurance the Most?

The policy can be a great choice for people looking for life insurance coverage who have less interest in cash value or investment. The biggest problem is that the premiums are not as flexible as other types of payments, so a person with a stable salary will be the best for this policy.

What Happens If Someone Wants To Close Their GUL Policy?

It is very unlikely that you will know your financial status after a decade or two. Financial situations change for the better and worse, and sometimes they come unexpectedly. There may come a time when a person who decided on this policy wants to end it mid-way through the payment process. By ending the policy, unlike the index universal life policy, you will have no money to take away from the policy, even if you are ending it yourself.

However, many insurance companies offer a partial or even full refund if you terminate the policy. This feature only is available after you have completed a certain number of payments.

After the specified amount of time has passed, such as 5 or 20 years, you will be able to get some or all of your premium payments worth of money back. This process is highly dependent on other factors set by the company, such as at what age you bought the policy, policy year, etc.

So, if you are interested in buying this guaranteed universal life insurance policy, be sure to check out all the details and build a detailed plan to deal with all kinds of possibilities before you buy.

Fact: The average cost of this policy is around $1 million for healthy, non-smoking individuals aged 100 and older. The average premium will cost around $1500-3000 per month.

Registered Index Life Insurance Policies

Registered Index Life Investments/insurance policies, or RIUL, is another type of universal life insurance. In this policy, the premium payments are lower, but there is a higher risk of the policyholder's cash value decreasing with market value. This feature can provide more value to the policyholder because the charges will have consistently lower rates than other traditional policies.

RIUL works similarly to regular IUL. The premium is saved in your account as the cash value, and the cash value is tied to the index of your choice. If the market goes up, so does your cash value. The difference is that when the market is down and not doing well, the IUL policyholder will not see a decrease in their cash value. However, in RIUL, there will be a limited decrease in their cash value. In return for this risk, the RIUL policies will have low-interest rates, low premium costs, and no or higher cap limits.

With RIUL policies, you can increase market participation and get more out of good market growth. Also, you can save a lot of money because you will be paying less than other premium holders. The RIUL provides all the features of a regular IUL but has a greater chance for growth and can become more valuable as a long-time investment.

RIUL is risky, but not as risky as variable Universal Life Insurance or VUL, which saves your money from going down extremely in the case of recessions or substantial index decreases.

Who Can Benefit from Guaranteed Universal Life Insurance the Most?

Someone that has more interest in investments and cash value will be more inclined toward this policy. However, RIUL should only be bought by individuals who can handle greater risk and are going into the policy with a long-term plan. It has the most opportunity for cash accumulation than other universal life insurance policies.

Fact: If someone directly invests in the stock market, there is a chance that they can lose all of their money. However, in RIUL, the loss has a limit; even in the worst of times, you will not lose all your cash value.

Variable Universal Life Investments/Insurance

It is one of the most popular choices for universal life insurance. Variable Universal Life Insurance, or VUL, is a type similar to a traditional IUL policy. It is a permanent life insurance policy with a cash value tied to an index. Unlike guaranteed life insurance policies, these are much more flexible with premium payments.

Variable Universal Life Investments/Insurance has sub-accounts in which a percentage of your cash value is tied for investment. These sub-accounts act similarly to mutual fund groups. As discussed before, directly investing in the stock market can reward you with great gains if you are lucky, but you could also suffer substantial losses. VUL gives the policyholder a bigger chunk of the market to take advantage of in favor of increasing their risk of losing their cash value.

Fact: Because VUL gets varying results, high to low profit and losses, from the investment part of the policy, it has gotten the name variable.

For the greater risk, VUL has the most flexible plans compared to all universal life insurance policies, along with very high growth potential. This is not provided in traditional IUL or even regular life insurance policies. However, because there is a greater risk involved, only people with high-risk tolerance should consider this policy.

How Does VUL Insurance/Investment Policy Work?

Like IUL, variable Universal Life Investments/Insurance has a savings component with a death benefit life insurance feature. This policy also has more flexibility and plans in terms of premium payments, and the premiums are saved into the savings account.

Fact: The savings account in VUL, and cash value in IUL are separate accounts that work differently.

The VUL savings consists of managing separate accounts, also known as “subaccounts.” As every year passes, the insurance company takes out the life insurance and administration charges and leaves the rest to be tied to the market to gain more profits. The working mechanism processes differently than previously explained IUL policy.

Two Components

The investment side of the policy in IUL is less risky and guarantees a profit, making the policyholder immune to market changes. In Variable Universal Life Investments, the life insurance company transfers the risk to the policyholder in return for getting more profits from the market.

Anybody who has an interest in buying this policy must remember that the sub-accounts may incur losses and, in turn, reduce the amount of savings one has. One significant or consistent loss can be detrimental to the entire policy and the person's savings. Suppose such an unfortunate case occurs in which both accounts are low on cash and cannot cover the cost of life insurance or administration. In that case, the policyholder will need to pay even higher premiums and rebuild their savings so that the account functions properly in the future.

Fact: Unlike traditional Index Universal Life Investments/Insurance, the company gives the risk back to the policyholder, and there is a chance of you losing your money and your life insurance policy because of bad market performance.

Sub-Accounts

All this talk of sub-accounts, but what are they? There is no need to worry, as they are just another component in this universal life insurance policy and nothing more. Consider separate sub-accounts like family or groups of mutual funds. Each account has a portfolio of bonds and stocks, along with other options of assets. Insurance companies have different rules when governing this part of the policy. They can put a limit on how many transfers the policyholder can do in a year, etc. If a person that buys this policy fails to understand the details and transfers more into the account and the account performs poorly in the market, then the person will need to pay a much more expensive premium from then on to cover the insurance costs.

Fact: Mutual funds are bundles of different stocks and bonds that are diversified in nature and professionally managed to prevent losses and reduce risks. To learn more about them, you can check out my book "Mutual Fund Investing on a Budget for Beginners."

Fact: A portfolio is the list of all the assets in a person's or an institution's possession, including stocks and bonds.

VUL is a more complicated type of universal life insurance policy that demands more administration work and labor. This is why the cost of management fees can range from 0.05% to a whole 2% sometimes, and these need to be paid every year. These sub-accounts work as mutual funds and, thus, are also considered securities. This means they have been regulated by FINRA-approved insurance providers only.

Fact: FINRA is short for the Financial Industry Regulatory Authority responsible for registering and licensing different financial institutions and ensuring they work according to the law.

The growth in these sub-accounts is tax-free, just like an IUL cash value. One could also take money out of this account by withdrawing or taking out loans. Unfortunately, the value of the savings needs to be above a specific level defined by the insurance company to prevent the premium costs from rising.

Fact: When a universal life insurance policy fails to pay more death benefits and management charges, its premium is increased. This sudden increase in payments is known as "Lapsing."

Is VUL A Good Investment?

VUL is a type of universal life insurance policy that is not suited for everyone but can be beneficial in some cases. When the market is soaring or is expected to perform well, this policy can give extremely high returns and great profits.

However, in times of turmoil and recession, the VUL policies will not be kind to the policyholder. The person needs to have a very high-risk tolerance and an appetite for investing.

It has risks and can give high results; however, the performance is not near to what a person can gain by directly investing in the market. This is due to the fact that the policy will take money out for death benefits and management charges every year, reducing the overall amount.

What Different Assets VUL Savings Are Invested In?

As explained, the sub-accounts of VULs act as a type of mutual fund group consisting of different assets and not just attached to one index, as in IUL policies. The investments options will range according to insurance companies, but most of them will offer the options below:

- Stocks
- Bonds
- Money markets assets
- ETFs
- Mutual Funds

- Guaranteed Fixed interest option, etc.

Fact: ETFs are "exchange-traded funds" that work similarly to mutual funds, being a bundle of different stocks. They are less risky and give more diversity to a portfolio.

Why Are the VUL Policies So Popular?

Among all the universal life insurance policies, variable universal life investments/insurance policies are the most feature-packed, which attract more people than others. There are four primary features that you can expect from this policy.

- A death benefit that can transfer wealth to your family

It is a viable life insurance option. After you die, the beneficiary of your choosing, this could be a family member or any other individual, can receive the wealth the policy has been collecting. This transfer of wealth to your future generations or loved ones is tax exempt and can help them pay for the funeral, covering their future expenses such as college fees or clearing out old debt.

- Have a savings account that you can take money out of in your times of need

You will not only be paying premiums for life insurance with almost no cash value, such as in guaranteed universal life insurance, but your money will be working as a financial tool to bring you more wealth in the future. This money is placed in the sub, where you can decide what assets to buy according to your risk tolerance. After a certain amount of payments and cash value has been reached, you will be able to take money out of this account anytime through different methods.

- Investments that have great potential for long-term growth

Variable Universal Life Investments/Insurance has a higher limit for growth than any other universal life insurance policy. They also have a chance of declining, but it is less risky than directly buying stocks on the market. If your cash value ever goes down, the premiums can be adjusted so you can still retain your life insurance.

- Flexibility in payments

Flexibility in payments is extremely convenient for policyholders and helps a person worry and stress less about making payments right on a date. You have the ability to adjust how much you want to pay based on the options given by the insurance company of your choice. You have the ability to change the dates, but they are not completely consequence-free.

Variable Universal Life Investments/Insurance policies are active as long as you are paying the premiums and fulfilling your end of the contract with the insurance company. Other types of insurance policies may also provide flexibility, but not as much as VUL. They allow adjustments in the timing and frequency of your payment and can even increase or decrease the amount in the present. Even then, your payments will be attached to sub-accounts to track asset growth.

Fact: People that find this policy attractive are high-income earners and retirees that buy this as an extra financial asset to add to their diversified portfolios.

Fact: The cost of VUL life insurance is higher than regular life insurance policies, so they should not be sought by people only looking for life insurance.

Advantages and disadvantages of Variable Universal Life Insurance/Investments

The first and foremost reason someone takes out a life insurance policy is to help their loved ones when they cannot defend and earn for them. Variable Universal Life Investments are a way to look out for your family members while adding more financial vehicles to their portfolios. They give you a greater chance of increasing wealth, which will ultimately help you reach your goals and help you do the things that you always saved up for. However, variable Universal Life Investments are extremely complicated, and they come with a higher level of risks which is not suitable for everyone. To find out if they fit you, continue reading and find out the advantages and disadvantages of this policy.

Advantages

Four main considerations make this universal life policy stand out among the rest and be worthwhile for the buyers. These are:

- The life insurance side gives a tax-free death benefit.
- The investment side provides a way for your money to grow tax free.
- The flexibility around payments within the policy means you control the timings and

amount you need to pay till the end of your contract.

- Lastly, you can change the coverage amount later in the policy.

Income Tax-free Death Benefit

Death Benefit is a way that you can transfer your life savings to your beloved family members after you pass away. If a person decides to transfer the wealth by a will instead, the money will be decreased due to tax cuts. Fortunately, with this policy, your family will receive the same amount of money you have left behind without any deductions. This money can be used to help them cover the debt, loans, funeral, and other expenses, which can allow your beneficiaries to not think about work when they are grieving. You can use this death benefit to support a charitable cause as well.

Income Tax-free Increase in Wealth through Investment

The potential to grow your money through VUL is much higher than other universal life insurance policies and simultaneously protects your money from extreme market crashes, which can cause you to lose all your money if you invest directly into stocks. This benefit is the main appeal of the policy, and the growth of your wealth in this policy is also tax-exempt. Your cash value will continuously grow; however, there is a chance of fluctuation.

Fact: Tax Laws are complicated within this policy. There are some exemptions in which the wealth might get taxed. It is important that before you buy this policy; you contact a tax advisor to help you best understand your contract's specifications.

Payments Are Under Your Control

It is heartbreaking when someone who has diligently paid for their insurance plan suddenly loses their life issuance coverage just because they missed one payment. Flexibility in the contract can allow you to control the time and amount of the payments, making sure that you do not miss them so that you can keep enjoying your life insurance policy till the end. You can pay more at the beginning and have the value slowly decrease over time. Vice versa, you can pay less at the beginning and slowly increase the value over time.

Fact: Any alteration in the original payment schedule will change the investment growth of your account. Big payments at the beginning usually mean your wealth will grow in value sooner.

One does not know how their finances will look decades from now, so having the option to change plans whenever possible is a great choice to have at the back. The two most important terms to remember are "Timing" and "Frequency." You will have reduced premium payments if you decide to slow down your payments and go with a low-frequency payment option. However, this will decrease the amount of money stored in your sub-accounts for your investments. Also, this kind of payment method may reduce the death benefit your children may receive. By decreasing the amount you pay for your premiums, you may need to pay for longer to meet the life insurance requirements. So, consider all the factors before changing the premiums in VUL.

Fact: You are allowed to add a large sum to your life insurance policy to increase the money in your accounts and reach the policy goals quickly. However, these transfers are subjected to tax rules, and the IRS can reclassify these payments governed by different rules.

Coverage Amount is Adjustable

In this policy, you have the ability to increase and decrease the value of your death benefit. Usually, life insurance companies do not give this ability to customers, and the buyers are stuck with paying a set amount for the life insurance and death benefit. However, with VUL, you can change this amount within specified limits. This, along with flexibility in premium payments and timing, makes the policy much easier to follow and complete. By the end, you will have enough value in your sub-accounts for a good death benefit for your beneficiaries.

Fact: Insurance companies have specified limitations and rules when it comes to VUL, and every company is different. It depends on the length of the contract and your age as well.

Disadvantages

Similar to advantages, four factors can make this kind of policy hard to pick. These include:

- Complicated rules
- Need for the increase in payments
- Time taken
- Unstable nature of the market

Complicated Rules

The complexity surrounding this policy can be off-putting too many new and unfamiliar buyers that do not want to spend too much time researching and understanding it. Whole life insurance policies and other universal life insurance policies have fewer complex rules and regulations. If you are someone that has a keen interest in buying VUL, it is essential that you be sure of the goals you are trying to achieve with it. You should be clear on how this policy will support what you want to do. Not only take time to evaluate your personal goals with the policy but also read the prospectus of the insurance company and have a meeting with a tax advisor.

Increase In Premium Payments

Variable Universal Life Investments/Insurance is expensive and will cost more than traditional life insurance or other universal life insurance policies. They will have higher costs initially, or you will need to pay them for longer.

In case of the market does badly and the value of the account goes below a certain level, there can be a sudden increase in payment amount in your upcoming premiums. These higher payments are there so that they can stand a market downturn in the future.

Longer Time Taken To Complete The Policy

You may think that all kinds of universal life insurance policies are long-term assets, which is to be expected. However, many people get into the policy for investing purposes. If you are the type of person intrigued by the investing side of the policy, remember to treat the returns as a long-term financial goal. They are not meant to be taken as a short-term investment option. If you want a quick investment stream to help you out, this is not the right choice.

There Are Market Risks Involved

The benefits of your investments potentially increasing with a higher limit come with the risk of your cash going down with the market. It is the nature of investments, stocks or bonds to fluctuate according to value and not be consistent. The premiums funding your sub-accounts will be tied to the market, and there will be a chance of them decreasing if the market performs poorly.

If the market goes down, the money in your account will decrease, which means you will lose your initial money gains. The extra money will need to be funded by higher premium payments. Failing to pay these higher bills will mean not only losing your investments but also your life insurance and death benefit.

Variable Universal Life Investments Compared to Different Policies

Multiple unique features set VUL policies apart from other options available. VUL itself is a very diverse plan with a wide range of choices. A person could choose and change the policy contract to make them more individualized to meet their specific goals. Unfortunately, these features do not come for free, and the buyer must pay higher costs for longer. They are more expensive than any other policy type, traditional and universal. However, this is still one of buyers' most popular life insurance choices. To know fully if this policy will suit you, here are some notable differences between it and its peers.

Term Life Policy and Variable Universal Life Insurance

Term life insurance policies are more common and known than Variable Universal Life Insurance Policies. They are the most common plan people are willing to get involved with. The main differences between them are:

- Term life insurance policy is only set for a smaller period, while VUL lasts an entire lifetime.
- Term life insurance policy only provides a life insurance death benefit. VUL provides a death benefit and an investment subaccount for the cash value to grow.
- Variable Universal Life Insurance Policies have no cap limit on their investment growth.
- Variable Universal Life Insurance Policies save and grow your money in an account as cash value. Term life insurance policy does not.

- In VUL policies, the buyer has a choice to tie their cash value with market-based assets. Term life insurance policy does not give this ability.
- Term life insurance policy premiums have fixed amounts and timings; they cannot be changed. In VUL policies, the amount and timings of the premium payments can be changed within a limit.
- VUL is more expensive than term life insurance because they provide more benefits and features.

Fact: Term life insurance is set for shorter times, e.g., 10-30 years, and is more affordable. Whole life insurance is for the entire lifetime and also has a cash value account. Term life insurance policy, unfortunately, has no cash value.

Whole Life Policy and Variable Universal Life Insurance

Many people pick term life insurance policies because they are cheaper and more affordable; however, whole life insurance has plenty of buyers as well. It is another extremely common option for the life insurance policy. There are many similarities between it and VUL. Both are complete life insurance policies that run for the entirety of a person's life. Also, they both have a cash value account in which money can be saved and potentially grow. The main differences between whole life insurance policies and variable universal life insurance policies are:

- Variable Universal Life Insurance Policies invest the cash value amount into different market assets in sub-accounts. Whole life insurance policies increase the cash value by adding a specified flat credited rate set during the purchase.
- Whole life insurance policy premiums have fixed amounts and timings; they cannot be changed. In VUL policies, the amount and timings of the premium payments can be changed within a limit.
- Coverage amount of VUL is adjustable and can be changed during the policy. Whole life insurance usually does not have this feature and has a fixed coverage amount that will be needed to be paid.
- VUL is more expensive than whole life insurance because it provides more benefits and features.

Universal Life Policy and Variable Universal Life Insurance

These two policies are very similar, and you may need to evaluate carefully which one best suits your needs when choosing what plan to buy and follow through the years.

Both are complete life insurance policies and have cash value accounts that grow the policyholder's wealth. The main differences between universal life insurance policies and variable universal life insurance policies are:

- Universal Life Insurance Policies do not have a self-directed investment account such as VUL. It, similar to a whole life insurance policy, increases the cash value through specified credited rates set by the company. These rates are chosen based on market interest rates.
- In Variable Universal Life Insurance Policies, a person can tie their cash value to stocks and bonds, while you cannot participate in a universal life insurance policy.
- Variable Universal Life Investments/Insurance Policies have much more flexible payment contracts, which can be adjusted accordingly. Universal Life Insurance also has flexibility in payments but has limits.
- Variable Universal Life Insurance and Universal Life Insurance both provide the ability to change the coverage amount of the policy. However, different limits are set for both to be able to change the amount.

Variable Life Insurance and Variable Universal Life Insurance

Variable life insurance is also very similar to Variable Universal Life Insurance Policies; however, they have key differences that can make a person opt for one over the other. Similarities are that they are complete life insurance policies, and both have cash value accounts tied to the market index.

The main differences between variable life insurance policies and variable universal life insurance policies are:

- Variable life insurance policies have less flexibility in their premium payment plan. They do not give the ability to change it very easily. They are set to be paid at a specified rate in a specific schedule. In contrast, variable universal life insurance provides more flexibility.

- Variable Universal Life Insurance coverage amount or death benefits can be changed and are adjustable. Variable life insurance coverage amount is also adjustable to a certain extent, but not as much as VUL.

Both variable policies have life insurance tied with investments. These sub-accounts are subjected to U.S. federal securities laws. It is well established that Variable Universal Life Insurance Policies are not for short-term investment gains. This is true for variable life insurance policies, too. If you cannot provide funding for it long term, do not sign for either of these plans.

Who will Benefit the most from Variable Universal Life Insurance Policy?

Whether this policy is right for you or not will be decided by your ability to pay for the policy, your ability to handle the increased risk tolerance, its ability to fulfill your financial goals, and the overall strategy of your financial planning. This policy is perfect for individuals looking for an extra investment vehicle with a death benefit who have well above budget for such an expense and the ability to handle the risks involved.

One must remember that even though VUL is a great investment tool, it is first and primarily a life insurance policy. If you pay your payments on time and fulfill the contract requirements, your loved ones can receive the death benefit at the time of your passing. Because the cash value is tied to accounts that will grow your wealth, the death benefit can reach a substantial value. You have the ability to take money out of the account when you are alive as well. All this growth and wealth transfer can be tax free as well.

It is a great policy and deserving of its popularity, but the risks and expenses involved are not to be overlooked. You need to carefully consider the pros and cons of every policy to make the best decision for yourself and your family.

Fact: Remember, if the assets in your investment part of the policy perform badly, not only will you lose money but also the life insurance. With small gradual decreases, the rate of your investment growth will continue to be stagnant or decrease, and the death benefit can also reduce.

Summary

- Indexed Universal Life Insurance is one of several universal life insurance policies.
- In Guaranteed Universal Life Insurance or GUL, you will receive a death benefit but almost no cash value.
- The advantage of Guaranteed Universal Life Insurance is that the premiums do not increase over time. However, the biggest disadvantage is that you can lose your entire life insurance and cash value if you miss your payment even once.
- If one wishes to close their GUL account for any reason, they can get a partial or full refund. However, this option is only available after substantial payments have been made.
- In Registered Index Universal Life Insurance or RIUL, you will receive a death benefit, and the policy will include a cash value account tied to the market index.
- There will be higher risks involved because the cash value can decrease with the downward trend of the stock market. However, it is less risky than directly buying shares, stocks, and bonds and buying a VUL. It is also cheaper than other universal life insurance policies.
- Variable Universal Life Insurance Policies or VUL are popular plans with more flexibility in

premium payments and higher growth potential than other universal life insurance types.

- They have very high or no upper cap limit, such as in Indexed Universal Life Insurance Policies. However, your cash value is subjected to market changes and can decrease if the investments do not perform well.

- The investment side of the policy works by using sub-accounts in which different investment vehicles can be added for cash value growth. These can include mutual funds, ETFs, etc.

- VUL advantages include; flexibility in payments, adjustable coverage amount/death benefit, tax-free transfer of wealth, and a higher chance of growth of cash value which a buyer can take money out of during their lifetime.

- VUL disadvantages include; complex rules, being riskier than other options, not being a good short-term investment vehicle, being more expensive, and the chance you will need to pay higher costs than initially planned.

- VUL is best for people will have high enough budgets to fund easily it's expenses and handle the risks.

Chapter 3: Are IULs What I Need for The Future

After discussing different financial life insurance policies, you may have developed a better understanding of Universal Life Insurance Policies and can now reach a decision on which policy to think about purchasing. However, to make an even more informed decision, you need to know more about indexed universal life insurance policies. By having all the information about their pros and cons, you can go into the policy with full confidence and fully be aware of the benefits and risks involved. With this information, you can assess if this policy is right for your future endeavors.

Elements of Index Universal Life Insurance/Investments

IUL is considered to be one of the better cash values providing life insurance policies. The money which you pay in premiums, a part of it, is stored and increases with the market gains, albeit with a specific limit of growth. However, this growth of wealth is tax free and your cash value will be protected by the extreme downward trend of the market, so you will never lose too much money, even if you are down on your luck.

Indexed Universal Life Insurance Policies are permanent life insurance policies that grant the policyholder full coverage, as long as premiums are paid regularly and other contract demands are maintained. During the policyholder's lifetime, the cash value increases as they pay the premiums. This cash value also grows with the market index over the years. The policy buyer can excess this money in diverse ways in the years before their death. The policy includes a death benefit, which can be transferred to your next of kin after your death, tax-free as well.

Unfortunately, the cash value growth component of this policy comes with a catch. The money here increases in value with the interest-based performance of the index you, or your insurance company, have chosen. The chosen index, e.g., the S&P 500, of the stock market determines how much money you will gain if there are gains to be seen. There is a chance that the index does not perform well and there is no growth of the cash value. If the index is down, you will have a low rate of return.

Fact: S&P 500 index in full form is the Standard & Poor's 500 index. In the 1900s, the index was first run by Standard Statistics Co. in 1923 and later merged with Poor's publishing company in 1941. The index started by following just over 200 companies initially, but now it tracks the 500 largest companies by market capitalization in the U.S. To learn more about stock market and its history, do not hesitate to check out "Decluttering the Stock Market by Magnus Carter."

Some companies do not offer any guarantees for the growth of the cash value, but some insurance companies do. However, these companies may demand higher premium payments in exchange. They may offer a limited but guaranteed rate of growth of your cash value so that it increases over time regardless of bad performance of market trends. Market fluctuation can only increase the rate, which means more returns, but not decrease it.

Even with this feature, the returns may not be great enough to justify the expensive premium costs for someone. Generally, IUL policies are considered to be riskier than other fixed universal life insurance policies, which also have a guaranteed rate of return at a lower premium cost. However, it is much less risky than variable universal life insurance in which you can directly purchase stocks and other market assets and also see your cash value decreasing.

Fact: Taking money out of your cash value during your lifetime is subjected to many rules and charges. You can borrow money from an index universal life insurance account, but failing to return will decrease your death benefit. Further details and methods of taking money out of the account will be discussed in later chapters.

Advantages of Index Universal Life Insurance Policies

After clearly understanding the basics of this policy, you may be more than eager to jump right into it. However, first, you have to determine your financial goals and whether the element of this policy aligns with them. It is also vital that before buying any permanent lifetime policy; you need to research thoroughly the policy's parameters and the best insurance companies in business that are offering it.

With that being said, here are some chief advantages to be aware of when planning out your financial future around an index universal life insurance policy.

A Chance of High Gains

Index Universal Life Insurance Policies have a system in which they take advantage of call options to gain more profits without necessarily increasing the risks of losing money. Other universal life and whole life insurance policies do not even come close to the gains that the index universal life insurance policies can make. The small interest credit gains they can provide are near to interest gains one can receive via a savings account at a bank, which is not even enough to keep up with inflation.

Fact: Call options is a contract in which the buyer has the right, not obligation, to buy a stock under specific conditions.

Fact: "Keeping up with inflation" means increasing the value of your money income, or savings, alongside inflation.

Although the returns in an IUL investment policy are not guaranteed and it is completely dependent on the market index values, the policy still guarantees some return so your money will have the chance of high returns, while receiving small, guaranteed returns, with no risks. As a long-term investment, this is far more beneficial as the index value increases over the years and the downward fluctuations are historically temporary.

Adequate Flexibility

Index Universal Life Insurance Policies are not as flexible with premium payments as VUL, but they are more forgiving than regular life insurance policies and other universal life insurance policies. They can be individualized in a multitude of ways to suit your financial needs and investment goals. You can practically design a policy yourself. A policyholder can change how much risk they can tolerate with investment options, change the cost of premium payments by adjusting the amount of death benefit the beneficiaries will receive, etc. One can even look into the policy riders and tackle an issue that worries them the most. For example, a person who is more concerned about age-related illnesses can choose a plan with a “long-term care rider” attached to it which can cover nursing home expenses in the late future. They can also attach an “accelerated death benefit rider” which can pay the expenses of doctors and hospitals in case of a terminal illness.

Fact: Index Universal Life Insurance Policies come with many customizable rider packages that target a specific need. These are often mentioned in the insurance company’s prospectuses.

Capital Gains are Free from Taxation

The gains or increases in wealth within the policy cash value will not be subjected to any kind of taxes. A capital gain tax is applied whenever a person gets a profit by selling stocks and bonds. It can even be applied when you gain money from other kinds of investments. Index universal life insurance policyholders, even when they see a massive gain in cash value, will not need to pay a capital gain tax, even though the money is tied to an index.

If a person takes out a loan from the account for any purpose, the money they receive is still not going to be taxed. It is important to remember that in order to keep taxes and charges from affecting too much, one must not take withdrawals before the policy matures. It is a benefit that you can take money out of the cash value at any time, but this should be treated as an emergency fund.

Fact: A policy matures when it reaches its expiration date, or the entire term of that policy has passed. A 15-year policy will mature after 15 years and the policyholder shall receive the policy's coverage amount.

The gains can be subjected to taxes if you abandon the policy before it matures. One may even need to pay taxes if they take out a withdrawal. This rule is similar to a 401k account or IRA, in which money can be taxed and penalties can be applied if money is taken out early. However, in 401k or regular IRA accounts, there are restrictions on how much money can be tied up with the stock market and have limited returns as a result. This does not happen in Indexed Universal Life Insurance Policies. Differences between these accounts and IUL will be further discussed later in the chapter.

Policy Does Not Affect Social Security Benefits

Social security benefits include a person receiving a certain amount of money when they retire. This is an important source of income for many in old age when they cannot work anymore. These benefits are available to people that have reached the age of 62.

These social security benefits are there to help you in your retirement age and should not be taken out before this time. Taking them early will shrink the overall benefit amount you will have, and you may run into financial hardships in old age, which is not ideal. Your social security benefits can decrease if you are taking out benefits and working simultaneously.

You can earn a certain limited amount per year after your retirement until they start to affect your benefits. However, with an IUL policy, you can increase your cash value wealth and it would not count as earnings that would affect your social security benefits. Any loan you take from the cash value account also will not be affecting your social security benefits.

If you need extra cash, you can take a loan out of the account and not need to declare it when applying for the benefits, which is a huge plus point.

A Good Death Benefit Amount

Index universal life investment policies are also life insurance policies that provide death benefits upon your death to your family. The costs of arranging a proper funeral and burial have begun to be extremely difficult to keep up with. This money can be used for your after-death expenses. The death benefit can help your children to pay off college loans, help your wife to keep up with mortgage payments, and cover other debt that might be hurting your loved ones.

The death benefit should be enough to pay for everyday expenses and beyond because of the accumulation process in this policy. If you do not take a lot of money out prematurely and timely pay off the loans that you receive from the cash value, your death benefit will be off a significant amount, such that your children and grandchildren might not have to worry about financial problems.

Additionally, when transferring this money, no cuts or taxes will apply and the entire money will go straight to your family members.

Fact: Experts suggest that a life insurance death benefit should be equal to 10-15 times the amount of your annual salary or full income.

Disadvantages of Index Universal Life Insurance Policies

No policy is a perfect match for everyone, as each person has different needs and goals. IULs are no exceptions and when deciding on whether to buy them or not, you need to understand their drawbacks very carefully and evaluate whether the advantages weigh more than the disadvantages in your financial situation.

It is important to remember that these policies are expensive and if you buy the policy when the market is going down, you might not see gains and only lose money by paying regular high premium payments. Your cash value will not be very beneficial in this case scenario. Moreover, if you miss your payments because you could not cover the high costs of the premiums, you could potentially lose your life insurance in the process and your investments.

Keeping that in mind, here are some other drawbacks to be aware of when considering buying this policy.

Limits on Investment Gains

As we discussed in the first chapter, there are participation rates that limit the growth of your cash value with investments. This participation rate can go as low as 25%.

Fact: Some insurance companies offer participation near completion 100%. So, if you are interested more in investing, consider researching companies available to you and which ones provide this feature.

On top of participation rate limits, there is a cap limit which is nearly 10-12%. This lowers the number of returns you will get on good-performing market years and you will miss out on substantial growth. These two restrictions together make the returns not very significant in short periods, even if those years have the best market performances. The only way you will see substantial growth with this policy is if you consider this only as a long-term investment and appreciate the life insurance part of the policy just as significantly.

Instead, if investing and money growth are your top priority and life insurance is not important to you, then it may be more beneficial for you to invest in the stock market directly. In this situation, consider variable universal life insurance policies because there are fewer limits on the growth of cash value. Checking your own financial stability and assessing your budget is the first step in figuring out your risk tolerance. If your investment/insurance goals and risk tolerance align with this policy after careful consideration, only then seriously think about buying the policy.

Insignificant Guarantees

Traditional life insurance policies have a guarantee on how much premium amounts will cost and predictable interest rates. However, this is not the case with index universal life insurance policies. IUL, similar to VUL, have unpredictable premium payments which fluctuate with market performance, although they have a limit in their range of fluctuation.

You need to have a high enough budget and appetite for long-term risk tolerance in order to ride comfortably out the up-down nature of premium payments. One year of bad performance in the market may offset your premium payments enough, such that you cannot pay them on time, and you will lose your life insurance in the process with your investments.

Lots of Convoluted Fees and Charges

There are plentiful different kinds of fees that come with the policy that may make you very frustrated if you ignore them or are oblivious to them. Some of the fees and charges included are:

- Premium expenses.
- Administrative costs.
- Riders' fees, if you choose to add riders.
- Commission fees.
- Surrender charges, in the case, when you want to close your account before maturity, etc.

The rate of gains in the index universal life insurance policy is already limited, and along with these fees, they may negate/nullify the returns altogether. You need to be completely satisfied with how much returns you will get and what coverage amount as death benefit your loved ones will receive when purchasing the policy. All the details need to be thoroughly discussed beforehand to avoid regret later in life.

Fact: More kinds of fees and charges are involved in this policy. We will discuss them more in upcoming chapters.

In short

Advantages of this policy include:

- Having a higher chance of receiving higher returns than other policies.
- The policies are flexible, meaning they can be adjusted to suit your budget, risk tolerance, and life worries.
- The capital gains are completely tax-free within the account.
- Social security benefits are not affected in any way because of the capital gains within the account.
- Higher death benefit which is tax-exempted during transfer.

Disadvantages of this policy include:

- Limits and capped returns.
- There are no guarantees of premium costs.
- There is no guarantee of high returns.
- Higher hidden expenses in the form of fees and charges.

Comparison of Life Insurance Policies with IUL

The main difference between traditional life insurance policies and IUL is that they are not investment vehicles and are not growing with the stock market index. In IUL, the investment side of the policy is entirely at the mercy of the index values.

Index Universal Life Insurance Policies require high premium payments to cover the costs of life insurance and the attached investment cash value account. They are one of the riskier types of policies, among other universal life insurance one could buy.

Mentioned below are the basics of all the life insurance options one could research before settling down on IUL.

Term Life Insurance

Unlike IUL, the term life is not complete life insurance and is set for only a few decades. This makes the cost of premiums more affordable and life insurance more accessible to people with less budget. This policy is also very straightforward, with no complicated fees and rules. It also does not have a cash value component and money is stored.

In this policy, you pay the premiums on time and if the policyholder dies within the set time limits, the beneficiaries will get the death benefit.

Whole Life Insurance

Whole Life Insurance, on the other hand, is a complete life insurance policy just like IUL. The policy matures at the end of the policyholder's life, while premiums are being paid on time. There is a cash value element in this policy, and gains are also seen. However, these gains are very low and are set at a specific rate.

The policyholder also enjoys not having to pay any fees and charges that an IUL policyholder would be paying with their plan. Unfortunately, whole life insurance policies are not adjustable, customizable, or flexible as index universal life insurance policies. In an IUL, one can change their rate of payment and the amount of payment as well while there is no option in whole life insurance.

Variable Life Insurance

As the term variable would suggest, the most advantageous feature of this policy is providing flexibility, even more than index universal life insurance. Unfortunately, more options for customization mean more rules and fees that make the plan more complex for the average person. The policy also comes with a cash value, but it can not only be regulated through stocks but also other securities, unlike IUL. If the performance of these securities causes a loss in the cash value, the premium payments will rise accordingly, which is a headache to deal with. If you fail to pay these suddenly increased payments, you will lose your life insurance as well. That is why the plan is riskier than IUL.

Fact: Variable life insurance and variable universal life insurance are two different types of policies. Be sure to not confuse them with each other as you read along.

Each policy can become the perfect policy for the right person. To find out if they are right for you, you need to look into your financial goals and limitations, and then look into different types one by one to find the perfect match for yourself.

This way you will make a well-informed decision about your finances and be sure that you made the right choice.

Is IUL a Good Life Insurance Policy and a Good Investment?

While the Index Universal Life Insurance Policy comes with many advantages that may align with the goals of many interested individuals however, this plan is not the best or even appropriate choice for the majority. The advantages do not come for free and one must be able to pay high premium expenses and also cover additional fees, which can be difficult to maintain.

The policy is for the entire lifetime, meaning you have to keep paying the payments regularly for decades, which is not suitable for most people. In the plan lapses, you may lose all the money you initially paid to the insurance company and also your coverage. People that have a lower risk tolerance and a lower budget, would be better at growing their wealth with stocks and bonds.

But, if you are someone who can handle the regular premium costs of this policy, then not only will you receive a good death benefit but also have insurance for other future expenses of life. If you can easily afford the plan, then it is a good policy to buy.

Fact: A life insurance policy "lapses" when you stop paying your premiums before it has matured. In this case, the policyholder will lose all the benefits and coverage. One can reinstate their lapsed policy under certain conditions, but this differs from company to company.

Fact: The "maturity" date of the life insurance is the date when the contract term has ended and the coverage amount is then payable by the insurance company. A life insurance policy is said to be "matured" when this date is reached.

401k Plan or Indexed Universal Life Insurance

One of the most popular ways American citizens save up for retirement is by using a 401k Plan to save and grow their money. It is a workplace or employer-sponsored retirement plan in which a person can constantly add a portion of their earnings into this account, which can then be accessed after reaching almost 60 years of age. A person can take money out of the account before reaching this age, but it comes with different penalties and deductions, similar to an IUL cash account.

That being said, there are many differences between the two plans.

- Contrary to IUL, there is no option to take the money out by borrowing or taking a loan against a 401k account to avoid penalties. The withdrawn money is also subjected to taxation in this scenario.
- An IUL policy is very different from a 401k Plan, primarily because the policy is life insurance and ensures a death benefit component which will be released at the time of death of the policyholder. This is not the case with 401k. The money saved in the 401k account will be given to the next of kin according to the account holder's will. Usually, the death benefit of life insurance policies will be much higher in amount than 401k savings.
- The premiums paid to the insurance company do not fully land into the account, but a part of it does. Then this part grows with the stock market. With a 401k,

the money fully lands in the account and stays there with no intervention from any companies.

- The cash value of IUL grows with the stock market index and companies can guarantee a return on it. However, there is no fixed growth of money in a 401k account.
- Index universal life insurance policy is a fairly risky investment asset, while a 401k is not related to any kind of investment. A person can use their 401k account to invest later on, but this is not the default state of the account.

Fact: 401k has restrictions on what stocks and bonds the account holder can invest in. However, unlike IUL, you will have full control of these investments.

- There are additional charges and fees involved in IUL policies, which makes it more complicated to understand. However, a 401k account works similarly to a regular bank account and there are much fewer fees attached to it.
- The money growing within 401k accounts with personal investments is tax exempt as well. However, whenever someone contributes or adds money to the account, they can claim tax deductions for that year. You cannot claim tax deductions with IUL premium payments.

Advantages of a 401k over IUL

Index universal life insurance policy and 401k both come with their share of advantages.

- In a 401k, you have the full ability to buy and sell securities.
- Your contributions can be matched by your employer as well, in many cases.
- IUL may come with additional benefits of death benefit and higher potential growth of your savings, but they require high regular premium costs and fees. In a 401k account, you can even not add any money to the account for years and still keep your account active.
- You can contribute any amount of money to your 401k account whenever you want. If you miss payments with the IUL policy, you can potentially use your cash value and all the coverage.
- There are no guarantees of gains in the account, but there are no risks of losing money as well. 401k investments are well diversified and have a low risk than directly buying stocks, which makes it unlikely for them to lose money.

Fact: 401k comes with a feature that allows your employer to add the same amount of money you separately paid into your account. This feature is called "employee match". This feature encourages people to make more contributions to their accounts as they will essentially be doubled.

Who will Benefit the Most from the 401k Plan?

401k Plan is suitable for every individual, mainly because it comes with no risk and is a reliable retirement plan. People who have no risk tolerance and are not interested in life insurance or investments can make a 401k account as soon as they get employed without any worries.

Roth IRA or Index Universal Life Insurance

Roth IRA, just like 401k, is another popular retirement planning account. An individual can save and grow their money as well through investing. However, the securities will be managed and chosen by themselves.

It is an account that only accepts your after-tax dollars, which allows the growth of the money through investment to be tax free. A person can regularly add a portion of their earnings, after paying their yearly tax, into this account that they can withdraw after reaching almost 60 years of age.

A person can take money out of the account before reaching this age, but it comes with a limit of $10,000 and one must be able to fulfill additional IRS criteria as well. However, there are many exceptions, and a person may take any amount of money out for specific purposes, such as buying a house or for paying medical bills. In a sense, it can work as an emergency fund.

It is one of the best investment tools to consider when thinking about retirement, but they are only available to people that have an income below a certain level. A person needs a history of earning their money through working with an employer, and not through pensions, investments, or properties.

Index universal life insurance policies and Roth IRA are both very good choices for retirement, but they are made for different types of people. If you decide to invest early with a Roth IRA and save a substantial amount there, you can live comfortably in your old age and even dabble in luxury combined with social security benefits. On the IUL side, the policy offers permanent complete life insurance coverage and also a cash value account that will grow tax free. After death, the heirs will benefit from a high death benefit and you have a probability of seeing substantial growth in your cash value account, which you can access before the policy matures.

Fact: Social security benefits are income assigned by the government in order to help workers to be self-reliant. They get paid at retirement or in any emergency.

Advantages of Roth IRA

There are many benefits of opening this account, some of them are:

- Saving and investing using a Roth IRA account saves you from paying taxes on the gains you will receive. After reaching retirement age, you can withdraw and transfer the amount of tax free as well.
- In case of emergencies, one can take money out of the account without any penalties, contrary to 401k and IUL. These withdrawals are also tax-free.
- After opening the account, you have the option to buy and sell your choices of stocks and bonds.
- Like 401k, investments are well diversified and have lower risk than directly buying stocks, which makes it unlikely for them to lose money.
- There is no RMD. RMD requires a person to take out mandatory withdrawals after reaching a certain age. In 401k, a person needs to take out a certain amount after reaching 70 years. However, Roth IRA has no such requirements.

Fact: RMD is the acronym for "Required Minimum Distribution." It states that owners of 401k, and other retirement accounts such as SIMPLE, etc, have to withdraw a minimum amount from their account after a certain age, currently set at 73. Failing to do so will incur heavy taxes on the savings.

Disadvantages of Roth IRA

Roth IRA account, while having many benefits, has their drawbacks too. Some of them are:

- People falling under the high-income bracket do not apply for the account. It is only available to low-income salary earners.
- There is a limit to how much money a person can add to the account. It is around 6-7 thousand dollars as of 2020.
- You need an income to apply for the account, but your employer will not match your contributions. Your contributions will not double annually with this feature as it does in 401k.
- There are no deductions you qualify for by adding money into this account, which you can get with 401k.
- There is a high 10% penalty if you generally want to take money out of the account.

Who will Benefit the Most from Roth IRA

The first aspect that will decide which policy will suit you the most is your budget. IUL policy is expensive and still comes with high risks in which a person might lose all their wealth, meaning it is only accessible to high-income individuals. On the flip side, one can only open a Roth IRA account if they are in the low-income bracket.

If you are a high-earning individual that wants a permanent life insurance policy and still wants to have the possibility to use the money when you are alive as well, then an IUL policy is the better option. Having more interest in investments and adding riders suggests you would be more inclined to purchase an index universal life insurance because it serves your financial needs.

However, if you are an individual that has a hard time with everyday finances, or are not interested in a life insurance policy in general, then opting for a Roth IRA account is a better option. The account is sufficient to maintain a good retirement income.

Every policy and plan we have discussed has its role to play in making a more diverse and well-rounded portfolio for investing and saving for retirement. If you have come to the conclusion that IUL is the best choice for you, after analyzing your needs and capacity thoroughly, then it is most important that you look into different insurance providers' prospectuses and note down the cheapest policy among them. You can even seek the advice of a professional to help or read the next chapter to get started.

Summary

- To know whether IUL policies are for you, first, you have to assess if the elements of the policy align with your goals.
- The elements that makeup IUL are that it is permanent life insurance, and has an investment component tied to the market that increases the chances of growing wealth to a certain limit, but is very risky and expensive.
- IUL's most attractive features are giving a high chance of potential growth, giving flexibility, a good amount of death benefit, etc. It does not affect social security benefits either.
- The most bothersome features of this plan are limits on investment gains, low guarantees, and various fees and charges.
- Term life insurance, whole life insurance, and variable life insurance all have their unique advantages but are very different from IUL.
- When shopping for a policy, you need to understand all the options and compare them to find what fits you the best. It is important to learn and compare IUL with other life insurance policies.
- 401k and Roth IRA accounts are both very popular retirement plan choices. IUL can also serve as a retirement fund, but there are many differences between them.
- 401k allows you to control your investments, have employers match your contributions, claim tax deductions annually, and require no permanent payment frequency.

- 401k is best for people that are just looking for a retirement fund and not fond of life insurance or investing.
- In Roth IRA accounts, one can add their after-tax earned money and even invest using it. No tax is applied to the investment gains and also withdrawals after retirement age. A person can take money out penalty-free in the case of emergencies before retirement age as well.
- Roth IRA is specifically designed for low-income earners that cannot afford expensive life insurance policies, such as IUL.
- After carefully comparing IUL with other options, if you have decided that this policy is for you, then the first step is to find good places to buy the policy from.

Chapter 4: Where Do I Go to Get An IUL?

After careful analysis, you might have made the decision to purchase an IUL policy to further your finances. But wait! It is not as simple. There are differences in costs and features and some company policies are better than others. You cannot just walk in a company building one day and expect to get the best IUL plan on your first visit. IUL policies are expensive, lifelong commitments which you might have to live with for the rest of your life. It is essential that one thoroughly research where to buy the policy from.

Dividing a clever strategy to figure out how and where you will get the best plan for this policy is of utmost importance. Taking out time to understand different IUL policies' benefits can save you thousands of dollars, in addition to guaranteeing complete satisfaction in the long run.

Strategy To Find Best IUL Plans

The insurance companies that offer IUL policies are not going to be equal and have differences in costs, rules, cap limit, etc. It is a shame that not every finance advisor and agent will know how to structure the best IUL policy, which not only gives a good coverage but also withdrawal benefits when the person is still alive.

By chance, if you come by a person with the necessary expertise, they will not be motivated enough to make sure you get the maximum profits out of this plan. Smaller insurance companies and agents may have difficulty looking at IUL as a retirement plan while also trying to manage the investment gains. You need to make sure that the policy that you are purchasing for retirement is best structured to cater to your needs.

One needs to understand that any policy you buy will come with its own nuances. You need to focus on all the contract variables and choose these variables wisely. The variables include the pricing models, the coverage amount, the fees and charges costs, legalities, expected outcome, etc.

IULs are not as popular as other retirement plans such as Roth IRA or 401k accounts, and even as a life insurance policy, it is not much sought out by the general public. If you are a wealthy businessman with personal finance workers, they can whip up a great IUL plan for you, but this luxury is limited to high-ranking business and finance officials. This is why you need to make sure that the broker, agent, or financial advisor you are working with is knowledgeable and has your best interest as their first priority.

Fact: Before you buy IUL, you will be given the entire plan for the policy. Make sure to invest time in making sure that the plan will give good returns, a good death benefit and also support many living benefits.

To ensure you choose the best option available, you need to follow certain steps.

Get The Cheapest Coverage Plan in The Market

Usually, when someone sets out to buy an insurance policy, they look for the plan that gives them the most possible coverage with the lowest premium values. It also aligns with common sense. Imagine a person walking into Liberty and saying that they will pay as much as they want for the least amount of coverage. You would be right to think they are insane. However, this is the kind of approach IUL requires. You need to get a plan that asks for more premiums, at least in the beginning years, and have the least amount of coverage.

The premium payments and the amount of death benefit/coverage your children will receive are regulated by the government. The insurance industry is under the eyes of regulatory authorities, so they follow the rules. Decades ago, when there were higher tax rates, people were looking at all the different ways they could avoid it. One way was to buy an extremely cheap life insurance policy, $5-10,000 worth and put 1 to 10 million dollars in the policy's cash value to avoid paying taxes on them. This was a commonly practiced scheme among the wealthy. It is clear that life insurance intended benefits were not being "invested" and there was some other nefarious purpose at play.

Soon the government got wind of this scheme and set new regulations. The U.S government passed bills which told the insurance companies that there must be a realistic balance between the death benefit and the price of premium one pays for the policy. It should, at least, be enough to keep the family of the policyholder from financial ruin and loss in the sudden case the policyholder dies.

To make a policy balanced, finance experts use several math calculations and formulas. After proper calculations, adding the factor of age, gender and health conditions, the minimum death benefit amount is found out.

Fact: Although many companies give options of policies in which gender is not taken as a factor. There is a gender gap between the costs of women and men when receiving life insurance.

Index universal life insurance policies work differently than regular life insurance policies, and the strategy to buy them is also different. You want to get the least coverage for the most premium. This means you can invest a lot of money through your cash flow account quickly, and these investments can grow as quickly as possible as well. Obviously, get the highest premiums in the range of your financial goals and risk tolerance.

It is more beneficial that you pay the amount you want to use as investments in the beginning period of 4-5 years. The plus side of this strategy is that your policy will start to gain wealth quickly, which then will be used for new investments in coming years and will give even more returns in the future.

You will start earning very good interest returns on an already big cash value and it will in a few decades become a pre-retirement, tax free source of income. The death benefit, which was originally very low, will increase due to the accumulation of investment gains and your heirs will be well-off in their lifetime.

Get Zero Floor on Loss

Paying your premiums means that you contribute to your cash value, which acts as an account. From the money stored in the cash value, you will be able to withdraw and transfer funds. To keep this cash value account secure, you need to make sure with your insurance advisor the percentage of the account, which will be tied to the stock market.

After determining the percentage, carefully select what kind of index the policy will be following throughout the years. Choose a well-balanced index that covers multiple industries and sectors.

Fact: Indexes that are well balanced means the index should have a diverse portfolio and, thus, have fewer risks of losses. Nasdaq Composite, Dow Jones, Russell Midcap, etc. and other indexes to choose from other than S&P 500.

After choosing a good index to follow, it is of utmost importance that many people forget to implement, set a floor of zero on losses. This means that the cap of loss or amount of loss should be zero end no money ever gets out even though markets are not doing well.

Using this strategy, the cash value will only increase in value. There might be times when the cash value stays the same for years due to recession, where there is no growth to be seen, but there will be no losses either.

Lock and Reset

Consider you have paid a fair share of your premiums and now this money has been in your cash value account, being invested and getting returns for the entire year. During this year, there might be a decrease in the returns. However, if gains are seen, then the profits you get from that year are added to the cash value. This new value is then used for investing in the future as the new principal. If you got a policy contract with zero floor loss as described above, then these profits will be saved from future losses forever. Because the profits that are now integrated with the principal never go down, we say that the profits are locked.

Fact: The principal amount is the initial amount of money someone has landed, invested or borrowed.

When the profits get locked, any decrease or poor activity of the index the next year will not take this gain away from the cash value. So, whatever happens, you will always have profits as a new principal and never go back to zero to climb back up again. With this feature implemented, even if a recession lasts for many years, the gains you get will not be hampered.

In other words, your cap will be reset as well. When the cash value is gaining, a percentage of the cap limit is utilized. Imagine getting 10% gains for the first year. Now, when the gains get added at the end, your cash value, with the new principal amount, starts from zero gain percentage and has the potential to get another 10% in the next cycle.

Fact: The beginning and end of the insurance cycle will depend on when you bought your policy. Whichever date you bought it, an annual cycle ends after 365 days.

Take care to understand this feature of your policy plan and make sure there are no exceptions or loopholes in this feature. It should be very clear that this is how the system will work.

Choosing Which Individual to Insure

Unfortunately, even though the topic of life insurance is not uncommon, many people do not know the fact that one can open policies for other family members' names. Do not forget this aspect when planning out an IUL policy. One can purchase a policy when they become 18 years old till the age of 85, after which life insurance companies will not issue any products to you anymore. If you are older, you can buy a policy of someone in this age bracket, provided that you are a close family member to this individual.

There are policies that one can take out on their newborn baby too, although there are several limitations and new rules to deal with. The size of death benefit and premiums also drastically change. In another scenario, a wealthy grandparent can open several accounts under their different grandchildren's name, adding money and letting it grow tax-free. Remember, when the grandparent dies, there will be no death benefit because the policy is for his grandchildren and not him.

Similarly, taking a policy out on your spouse, siblings or children's name is an easy process. There are different pros and cons to consider. However, if your children's future financial security is the main purpose for the account, then opening one in their name is the best move.

Find the Best Insurance Provider

Plenty of insurance companies that are willing to sell IUL policies, but how do you decide which one to choose from? Well, all of them have variations in their policy guidelines, differences in rules, etc. After understanding what you want your policy to do, you can then compare the different options and shortlist them to pick from. It is a good idea to ask an advisor for their opinion on the different policies and to list the pros and cons of each. Their advice should be clear and to the point of making your decision-making process easier.

IUL is a huge commitment, so do not shy away from asking in-depth questions and getting long, but clear explanations. You should approach the topic with an attitude of getting the best deal out of your investment and nothing less.

The investment advisors and company employees may complicate the aspects of the policy with jargon, so continue asking questions until you are completely satisfied why one option is being recommended over the other. There is no room for error when planning for retirement. Do not hesitate to walk away if the plan they are proposing does not match with your goals and tastes. There are plenty of policy providers to choose from, so do not "settle" or "compromise" with any.

Ensure Frequency and Cost of Payments Appropriately

There will be an order in which you have to pay expensive premiums and making sure that you pay them so that your policy does not lapse is very important. Do not forget the strategy of paying more costly premiums at the start, however, it should be within your reasonable budget range. Ensuring a good premium frequency order will help you not miss payments and also give you the target returns which you desire.

If done right, you may be earning a good amount of interest gains and accumulating wealth in your cash value in just 5-10 years.

The first thing to do is to figure out all the timeline options to choose from. Select the one that you are most comfortable with and confidently know that you can contribute the required premium payments at those times.

There are different timeliness and frequency of payments that also affect when you will be able to make withdrawals or loans against your policy. Be aware and comfortable with those dates as well. At this point, learn about the surrender charges and other costs involves with the policy in the case of an emergency. Many companies give a grace period, in which you have delayed your payments, but the policy would not lapse. Remember to ask about the grace period too.

All these answers should be available to know before you buy the policy, and timelines are one of the most important factors to be crystal clear on. If planned right, these considerations will maximize your profits and you get to the point quickly when you can start borrowing and withdrawing.

Fact: Be extra sure about the point when you will get to withdraw money from the policy's cash value. The closer the point, the better. You can then use this money to fund your or your child's wedding, fund a down payment for a house, etc.

Important Terms to Understand

To make sure that you easily follow along the conversation with the insurance company and advisors, and be able to decipher the policy layout, you will need to understand some important industry specific terms, along with the ones that have already been mentioned.

Floor Rate

The floor rate is similar to "Cap Limit', only on the reverse. The floor rate limits the amount of loss a cash value or sub-account will lose when the market is doing poorly in IUL. It can also mean the minimum amount one can gain in the case of GUL.

The floor rate in IUL should be usually at 0%, which prevents the money from decreasing in value if the market goes down to less than zero. However, there will be some cuts in your cash value because it has to cover the costs of account fees and administration charges for this negative performance year.

Sometimes, there might come an IUL policy which offers a guaranteed floor rate that is above 0%, which means you get at least 1-2% gains, or whatever the floor rate is, even if the market performs poorly and the index is going down.

Floor rates are extremely important in a policy because they limit the number of losses and reduce the risks associated with the plan. It is an important factor to be attentive off, even though the potential to gain is the reason why people buy the policy in the first place.

You also must pay attention to the "Cap rate" and "Participation rate" alongside the floor rate to fully grapes what your account will do in different situations. The limit of gains available because of the policy is determined by them.

Dividend Interest

When a person buys stocks and shares in a company, after a specific time, normally one year, the company gives a portion of their profits to your account based on how many shares are in your possession. This takes up a significant portion of yearly returns when directly buying stocks on the stock market. However, it is important to understand that the index universal life insurance policies do not add dividends interest in your account, even though the cash value is following the index.

The cash value grows because of the increase in the index values. This might be a turnoff for many people because the return percentage for an index, similar to S&P 500, is around 2.5%. You will miss out on this type of return with IUL policies.

Volatility Danger

Risk is a big part of the policy. Because of how the policy account generates growth, by adding interest to the cash value based on index values, the returns are subjective and not an assurance. However, paying your premiums so that new investment stocks or bonds are being bought is a must.

Volatility indicates that the index can go through drastic changes, positive to negative and vice versa, relatively quickly and without warning. You might need to pay even more in the future if the performance is continuously bad. Also, an insurance company has the ability to change the cap limit and participation rate in these situations, so that they can keep a profit margin for themselves.

Top Insurance Companies to Buy Index Universal Life Insurance Policies

There are many insurance companies to choose from, but some are better than others and are providing better policy plans, services, and extra features. IULs are a popular section of life insurance companies, and many are constantly evolving to stand out from their competition.

The companies listed below are chosen based on their:

- Policy performance.
- Financial Strength.
- Flexibility
- Policy Options.
- Customer Services, etc.

That being said, the most popular choices of IUL providers are:

AIG

AIG stands for "American International Group". It is one of the top insurance companies that operates globally with a hundred years of history. It is the largest commercial insurer in the USA and Canada.

American National

American National began in 1905, and currently has a market cap of $3 billion dollars. It is one of the top companies for life insurance, and also provides a variety of IUL policies, along with other life insurance plans.

AXA Equitable

AXA Equitable or Equitable has been ranked one of the best insurance companies in the world, giving great options in retirement plans and life insurance. It began in 1817 and has over 200+ years of history. It has gotten only a few complaints in recent years, all resolved.

John Hancock

This company is also among the best in the world. It has over 90 Comdex ratings, and solid ranking all around. It provides two unique approaches in its life insurance plans to attract more consumers. They are:

- John Hancock Vitality Program
- Express track underwriting

In the Vitality Program, policy holder's premiums are decreased based on healthy habits which they can prove using Fit Bits, Doctors visits, etc. With their Express

Program, a person can acquire life insurance within 3 days without an in-person doctor's checkup.

Fact: Comdex is a popular and well-recognized rating system that quickly shows the financial strength of a company.

Lincoln National

Lincoln National Corporation runs the Lincoln National Insurance Company based in New York and is also ranked among the best of the best. They have one of the best universal life insurance options among all the companies and provide a unique underwriting program as well, in which you can get life insurance without a medical exam.

Minnesota Life

They are among the life insurance companies that do not get talked about in mainstream conversation much but have a great product line, especially with universal and other non-conventional life insurance policies. They have been operating for 150 years. They can be bought from anywhere in the country except New York, where they operate under Securian Life Insurance.

Mutual of Omaha

Mutual of Omaha and United Omaha Life Insurance Company are among the top insurers operating in the U.S. Their Comdex rating is above 90 and have a good score in other rating systems as well. They offer unique policy designs that may cater to your individual needs, which you cannot find anywhere else in the market.

National Life Group

National Life Group Insurance Company is primarily a mutual insurance company, but they offer a variety of flexible packages and policies, including IUL. They began their business in 1848, giving them well over 100 years of experience in the business. They provide two types of IUL policy design:

- Option A, in which death benefit is fixed.
- Option B, in which death benefit also grows with the cash value.

North American Company

This company has been operating for more than 100 years and provides a variety of options in term life insurance and universal life insurance products. Among the top insurance companies, it offers one of the most affordable life insurance policies for people with various financial and life circumstances.

Among the IUL policy options, Rapid Builder IUL and Survivor GIUL stick out the most. Rapid Builder quickly grows money in cash value and survivor GIUL is life insurance made for two people while asking for only one premium payment schedule.

Pacific Life

It is considered among the best global insurance companies and has over 150 years of experience in the business. The company is mostly recognized for its dividend-paying life insurance and index universal life insurance policies. It offers unique IUL plans, including one with more emphasis on real estate.

Penn Mutual

The company is usually the first pick when considering any cash value providing life insurance. They are an innovative business, with their famous IUL and dividend-paying whole life insurance policies. Their dividend payments go up to 6% and even more. By being innovative, they have certainly not compromised on their stability and have extremely high ratings, including 90+ in Comdex. They also offer an underwriting policy program in which an account can get approved within 24 hours, without a medical check-up by the company.

Fact: It usually takes 1-2 months for the approval process when applying for any life insurance policy, especially a permanent life insurance plan.

Prudential

Prudential Financial Company is one of the family branches of the Prudential brand, which has become a global giant. It offers one of the best variable life insurance policies in the market, but its IUL policies are quite excellent as well. It was established in 1875 and has strong ratings across the board.

Symetra

This is a relatively new company, having been open for only 60 years, but it is backed by the Japanese leading insurance company "Sumitomo Life" which has over 100 years in the business. It has very good ratings including Comdex, but not as good as its competitors. However, there IUL products are not to be underestimated when buying a life insurance policy.

They offer 9 different index strategies to choose from, with three different death benefit options and 3 indexes to tie cash value with. There is also an above 0% interest guarantee with some rules applied. The best part is that one can start withdrawing from the account only after one year of opening.

Transamerica

It is one of the innovative life insurance companies that offers one of the best cash value life insurance, whole life insurance, and index universal life insurance policies. The company has over $1 Trillion in life insurance in force currently. They have a good competitive rating score as well.

There is no one "best" life insurance company for IUL that suits every person. The best policy is the plan that fulfills all your goals while maintaining your budget and appetite for risks. To determine which plan is the best for you, you need to compare each company's IUL plans with each other.

Fact: "A.M. Best Ratings" is a rating organization that is dedicated to rating life insurance companies. They were founded in 1899 and are widely accepted. All the companies mentioned have an A or A+ rating on this scale.

Index Universal Life Insurance Policy Marketing

Imagine you are sitting on your couch thinking about buying an IUL policy and suddenly an ad for IUL starts playing on your TV They are listing all the benefits and talking about their company, and you feel that it may be worth looking at. However, it is advised that only extremely stable and financially strong companies be considered buying these policies.

Many negative remarks surrounding IUL policy in the insurance market mostly are because of bad marketing. Index Universal Life Insurance Policies are not going to work as an investment plan. They should be considered a life insurance policy first.

Models of Performance

Index Universal Life Insurance Policies are attractive to people looking for an advantage in their stock market. Many want to diversify their portfolio of assets by including IUL in the mix, and insurance companies know this as well. Thus, when companies hire marketing teams, they instruct them to show their products as an investment vehicle. In these cases, the product that is being sold, and IUL policies, do not match the expectations of the buyers and this creates a deceptive environment for the consumers.

This is mostly seen in advertisements where the policy is only showing the material benefits and wealth growth within the cash value of an IUL when the market performance is positive and does not talk about the risks and drawbacks associated with bad index performance. It is not realistic to think of life insurance policies, or any financial services, from an idealistic point of view. The truth is that the market is extremely volatile, increasing and decreasing based on hundreds of factors, and no one can predict 100% predict what annual returns will look like a year later.

For example, you have bought an IUL plan with a 12% cap limit. Imagine the market index has risen 24% in the last two years since you bought this policy. You may expect to see a 24% increase in your wealth as well, however, your account has only seen a growth of 12%. This scenario can occur one year before the index grows 24% and the next year does not show any growth at all.

Now add on the other limiting factors of the IUL policy in the scenario. Imagine you only have a 75% participation rate with your policy. Then, even if the market has risen significantly, you will only see 9% returns after 2 years. If you would have invested directly, it would have been 24%.

This is why one should always be aware of personal goals. If the direct investment is more important to you, and you are not particularly interested in life insurance, then this policy is not for you. If you are clearly interested, remember to set your goals within realistic expectations and know about all the drawbacks and limitations and be comfortable with them. Be fully satisfied with the plan you are buying and not get swindled by deceiving advertisements.

Fine Print

Another big complaint and reason for dissatisfaction with the IUL policy is the lack of disclosure about different charges, and fees and, most importantly, about the insurance company's power to change the participation rate and cap limit rate at different times.

As mentioned once before, the cap limit and participation rate, which the companies may boost, are not a guarantee and can even be changed after one year as per the company's rules. The advertisements of these companies may give hypothetical estimates of you growing a substantial amount of money, 10-20x in a cash value account, but they will be misleading. The insurance company can change the rates that were mentioned to you before, and oy receive a fraction of what they claimed before.

In addition to misleading data, hypothetical analysis can also hide the cuts your account will go through for policy fees. When the market is not performing its best, you will actually see a decrease in your wealth in an IUL account, and you will need to pay more premiums to cover the losses, even if the floor rate was mentioned to be 0%.

Understanding all the factors that go into making the policy before buying a permanent life insurance plan like IUL is extremely important. The policy's future with good performance, bad performance, and everything in between should be clear to you.

How Much do Index Universal Life Insurance Policies Cost?

Premium payments of your index universal life insurance policy will depend on numerous factors, which can change the rates drastically.

First, you will need to speak to an insurance advisor or a life insurance agent and establish your goals with them. Whether you want to focus more on the death benefit and life insurance side of the policy, or the cash value investment side? It will help them devise or pick a plan that is more suitable for them, and each plan will cost differently.

Then, there are options to add riders or additional benefits. If you decide to add any rider, such as a term insurance plan, chronic illness, etc., then you will be charged extra for them.

Fact: Each insurance company has its specific riders which can be applied to any of their life insurance policies, including IUL.

Another essential factor for determining the premium costs of your IUL plan is the type of death benefit options you will choose. As mentioned above, different companies provide a variety of death benefit options, with different designs, and all cost differently as well. Usually, a fixed death benefit will cost less in premium payments, and increasing a death benefit will consequently cost higher.

Index Universal Life Insurance Policies have great flexibility. This just does not mean ease in premium payments, but also indicates the number of variations the product has to accommodate as many people as possible. They have a lot to offer and should be strategized accordingly to provide a well-rounded, worry-free generation of wealth.

How to Open your IUL Account

After discussing all the places where you can get an IUL policy and how to avoid buying a bad policy, it is time to discuss the steps of opening an IUL account.

Index Universal Life Insurance/Investment Policies are made to fit your goals and can be customized in various ways. In order to get the best experience before applying, be clear on the fact that you want this policy and accept it with all its risks attached. Also, do not skip looking at different companies' IUL policy designs to see which one is the most beneficial for you.

Step 1: Know your Wants

Many people will look into the policy and be motivated by profits to sink their time and investments in it, only to realize that it was not something they wanted. It is crucial to know what you want your goals to be, and especially know what you want your policy to do for you.

Being sure about your goals will protect you from regrets as well. If you are not clear about your goals, then you should not be buying any financial services.

Decide whether you want a higher death benefit or a higher cash value. Decide what problems you worry about the most so that you can buy riders to counteract those worries about the future. After you have your priorities set, then you can move forward.

Step 2: Know your Needs

Maybe you are the type of person who understands what they want, but not what they need. You have to take time out of your busy schedule and figure out what you actually need based on your financial situation and background. Without careful assessment of your situation, you should not buy any type of life insurance.

Based on your life and background, you can determine the minimum amount of death benefit you will require for you and your family. You need to choose an amount that you can pay the premiums for. If you need more coverage than you can afford, consider getting a term insurance rider to bridge this gap.

Step 3: Find a Broker

Finding the best insurance company and the best broker you can is also very essential and for good reasons. Most people, and maybe you as well, slowly have their homes, cars, businesses, and lives insured by the same company. It might be due to loyalty, convenience, or being satisfied with their services. Some buy from the same insurance companies as their parents. Regardless, shopping for the best insurance plan has a lot at stake. Having a seasoned insurance broker helping you along the way can be the deciding factor in finding the best company and plan for you. They can help you access many companies, help you design a plan for you, and even find the best prices on the market.

All IUL policies of different companies are going to be different in one way or another. Just as with any other product, be free to shop around and spend as much time as possible to find what really suits you and be sure to add a broker to help you along the way.

Step 4: Select an IUL Account

The insurance agent or broker will present you with different options of IUL packages from different companies and have you go through them or discuss each plan's unique feature with you. Once you evaluate many policies, pick the one that suits your wants and needs the most.

Once selected, your broker will handle the rest. You will be required to go for a medical exam, and blood and urine tests for insurability requirements. You will also be presented with the necessary paperwork which you will need to read and sign. And then your account will be opened within the time frame given by the company.

After opening your IUL account, you will start paying your premiums and see your cash value grow with time. You will be able to check your growth and be rest assured that your beneficiary's life will be paid for with your life insurance. However, there may be times when you might need to take money out of the policy.

Summary

- There are many companies to buy the IUL insurance policy from, but finding the best one will take some planning.
- Strategy to find the best plan includes searching for the cheapest coverage plans so that premiums are low.
- Having 0% floor loss, and bad market index performance does not eat up your cash value and your premiums stay down.
- Having your policy work with a lock and reset mechanism, so that previous years' returns never get lost.
- Deciding what person needs the insurance which can provide the best possible outcome for your family.
- Finding the best insurance company to buy your plan from.
- Paying a higher amount of payments on premiums in the beginning year of life and allowing your cash value to grow quickly.
- Some of the best insurance companies on the market to buy IUL policies are AIG, American National, Lincoln National, etc.
- All the companies listed are top insurance companies in the U.S., which have unique policies and riders.
- IUL marketing can be misleading, so be wary about advertisements and schemes you see in the media. Only buy a plan after thoroughly researching the specifics yourself.
- Opening an IUL is an easy process, in which you need to figure out your priorities, figure out what are

your limitations and needs, find a broker, and then fulfilling the insurance company's requirements.

Chapter 5: When to Cash Out?

After you have successfully set up your IUL account, you will need to pay the premium payments on a regular schedule until it matures. After maturity, after your death, your family shall receive the coverage amount. However, IUL policies are not just providing life insurance, they also provide a cash value account. In this account, your money accumulates as years pass by and you can then use this money to achieve your life wishes. After your wealth has crossed the specified amount, you can then start to take money out.

Insurance company's operations differ from each other and some may allow you to start cashing out after some amount of payment or after a specific time period. If you want an account that allows cashing out sooner or later, make sure to add them to your goals and design your IUL policy accordingly.

IUL Policy at Death

Index Universal Life Insurance is a cash-value account and is not only meant to be utilized at death. The built-up wealth is meant for the policyholder to use during her/his lifetime. **After your death, only the death benefit/coverage will be**

transferred to your beneficiaries, and not the money saved in your cash value account. The wealth in the account will revert back to the insurance company.

If you want to include also cash value account transfer with the death benefit upon your passing, you can definitely find many IUL policies that are designed to do so. Unfortunately, they will cost more compared to only coverage payout policies.

Methods of Cashing out

There are several methods by which a policyholder can take money out of their IUL, or any cash-value life insurance account. These are:

Withdrawals

As a policyholder, you are able to withdraw money from your cash value account, however, the amount of funds you want to transfer will have to be equal to the amount you have paid as premiums.

Fact: The amount you have paid through premiums, and you can withdraw, is known as the "Cost Basis".

Because it is technically the money generated by your income during your early life, they are not taxed and carry no charges during the process. Unfortunately, you have to pay taxes on the gains of the policy earned in the cash value.

Fact: The money you pay your premiums with comes from your salary or business income. You probably have paid your income tax on this amount, so there is no need for it to be taxed again.

Many policies allow withdrawals to exceed this limit. In this scenario, you can take more money out without paying charges to the insurance company, but you will have to pay taxes on them.

Another important factor to keep in mind is that withdrawals will decrease the amount of the death benefit. If you want to keep your life insurance coverage to give the exact amount to your beneficiaries as decided, then you should not cash out with withdrawals.

Loans

The policyholder can easily take out loans or borrow against their IUL insurance policy. Usually, when you apply for loans from a bank, they ask for your credit score, and you have to go through a rigorous process of application. Contradictory, you will not need to go through any of the hassles with IUL loans, essentially because you are borrowing money from yourself.

However, there are interest rates that need to be paid, although they will be lower compared to the market interest rates at the time. So, what happens if you do not pay back the loan? In this situation, if you die before the loan is paid back, the balance is going to be deducted from the death benefit.

Surrender

Almost every life insurance policy can be surrendered, which just means canceling your policy before dying. When you cancel your policy, you will receive the cash value amount. However, an expensive surrender fee will be charged on them. You will also not receive any coverage amount, neither will your family even after your death. You are basically surrendering your coverage amount despite paying for however many scheduled premiums.

Unfortunately, you will also need to pay taxes on this amount that is above the aforementioned cost basis.

Life Settlement

If you ever decide that you do not want your IUL policy anymore, there is a way to sell it and get money from a third party. This method is called a life settlement. The person you sell it to will be the one giving you money as a onetime cash payment. Often, this cash payment is more than what you might get than the same account's surrender value.

After the policy is sold, the remaining premiums will be the new policyholder's responsibility and they will get life insurance coverage when they die. You will not have any connection to the account anymore.

Fact: Insurance companies are extremely wary of fraud. The company has the right to cancel your entire policy if they find any international dishonesty from you as a policyholder. To counteract fraud, insurance companies will also go through an investigative period after your death to determine that no foul play occurs.

Surrendering your IUL Policy

When to Surrender?

To completely access your cash value account, you might be considering the option of surrendering your policy after substantial wealth has been built up. But why would anyone surrender a life insurance policy in the first place? Life does not always take a straight course, and you may have to live through such scenarios which call for such drastic actions.

Here are some reasons why a policyholder might want to surrender their IUL policy.

- Better Opportunities

Normally, this is not a common scenario because not only does life insurance expenses increase with the more you age, but also there is an increase in costs with more health issues as well. However, there is a possibility that you may have found a better, more beneficial, or more affordable policy plan than the current one you are already on.

It can be due to many reasons. For example, years have passed since you last smoked or your health has become better than when you bought the policy.

In these situations, it is very beneficial to shop around for some new IUL policies at a lower cost. Before transitioning from the policy, be sure to check that the new policy has been accepted and running smoothly before ending your current one.

Switching other accounts is not a new technique. Before buying the life insurance policy, look into the 1035 exchange and see whether you are eligible to apply for it. This scheme can save you from paying taxes.

Fact: Section 1035 of the tax code allows policyholders to transfer money from one life insurance policy to another without any taxation on the process.

- Difficulty in Keeping Up with the Payments

Any permanent life insurance is an expensive ordeal, and IUL being a cash-value account, is even more expensive than the standard prices. Perhaps during planning, you might not have taken into consideration the significance of the premium payments and cannot handle the policy taking a big chunk of your salary every month.

There might be a chance that you change your mind about IUL and want to switch to more affordable options, such as term life insurance. If you believe term life insurance is enough to fulfill your financial goals, then you may see no need for an expensive IUL policy being in your possession.

- No Need for the IUL Account anymore

Again, life circumstances may differ from what you expected, and there could be scenarios where the reason for buying life insurance in the first place is no longer in your life. You may just decide that the policy is not helping your goals and want to end it.

For example, imagine a dependent that was fully relying on your source of income to live, but now can sustain themselves and does not need your help anymore. In this scenario, you may be wanting life insurance coverage to support them, but now, it is not needed.

- In Need of Quick Cash

You may find yourself in a conundrum in which you might need a large amount of money quickly. Maybe you have a major expense to deal with or have spotted a better investment opportunity that you want to dabble in.

You can also run out of liquid assets if your income has suddenly stopped and want to cover life expenses from then on with the cash value account.

Many people take money out to fund their first home purchase and deal with medical bills. In these cases, selling or surrendering the policy seems like a good option, and even more so if the need for life insurance is also diminished.

Calculating Surrender Value

Surrender Value is the amount you will receive after you have successfully surrendered your IUL insurance policy. This will be the amount of cash value after surrender charges have been cut from the account.

This value is based on how much money did the policyholder pay as premiums during their entire life that went into the cash value account. They will also receive gains/returns they have earned through the index growth. From this wealth, surrender charges are cut. If any loans have been taken against the policy, the value of this loan will also be deducted if the amount is not paid back yet.

It is important to remember that during surrendering, only the cash value accounts will be transferred. This might cause a problem because a relatively new account takes time to build money in this account and even more time for it to grow significantly. By surrendering early, there might not be much money in the cash value account.

As time passes and the policy gets closer to maturity, the surrender fees/charges also decrease. Some companies completely make surrender charges obsolete after a certain period. You would want to reach this point before surrendering your policy. It will be an ideal time because your cash value account may have significantly grown as well.

Moreover, surrender value is not completely tax free either. The amount you will receive above the cost basis will be taxed. Income tax laws will be applied to the difference.

Remember that if you surrender your policy, you will lose your death benefit and coverage of the life insurance completely. If life insurance or providing a safety net for your family is a primary concern, do not hesitate to discuss different options with your life insurance broker or agent. It is an equally important task to figure out your financial needs and goals during this process as well. Depending on your reasons, your broker may find you a better solution than surrendering.

Taking Out Loans from Your IUL Policy

How Much Can You Borrow?

This depends on the policy type and insurance company that you have bought your policy from. The policy's specific terms can also change the parameters. The amount of money that a policyholder is allowed to loan is different for each of them, generally.

Fact: You can borrow from several different types of life insurance policies and not just IUL. You are allowed to borrow from your cash value in adjustable life insurance, whole life insurance, variable life insurance, and variable universal life insurance, among many others.

Fortunately, you can easily find life insurance policies allowing loans up to 90% of your cash value account, if that is what you are looking for.

For example, if you have $200,000 in your policy account, then you can be allowed to borrow nearly $180,000 without much hassle. If you have $50,000, you can take out as much as $45,000.

Taking out a loan means that you will need to pay extra money in the form of interest, according to the interest rate set by the policy, on top of the borrowed amount.

Because you want to have the interest low, you will need clear planning in order to pay back the loan quickly. For example, you took out a large sum from your account for paying your mortgage but did not have a plan to pay it back. The large sum will start to accumulate high interest as time passes on, which could have been avoided.

When a person decides to not pay back their loans in their life insurance policies, the amount is then deducted from the coverage amount. However, if the interest rates are high and are stacking up, increasing the total value of the loan.

If the total amount you have to pay back exceeds the death benefit, at this point, the insurance company has the right to cancel your life insurance policy completely.

How Life Insurance Loans Work

Having a set of money to take out loans from is a great way to get a hold of cash, but loans have their own advantages and disadvantages and may not be suitable for every situation.

You have to weigh the pros and cons of taking out loans from your policy before borrowing money. Here are some key factors to keep in mind:

- Coverage Value will go Down

Even if you took out the loans intending to pay them back, the coverage amount will decrease if you died without doing so. Your death benefit will be reduced by your loan's amount, the original borrowed amount plus the interest.

For example, you have bought life insurance that offers $100,000 coverage. Years later, you take out a loan of $30,000. Until you pay back these loans, your family at your death will receive $70,000, which is less than the coverage amount that you bought the policy.

- Interests Rates

Unlike the premium payments, you will not receive monthly or yearly premium bills. The insurance company does not set a loan repayment schedule and even does not require that you pay back the borrowed amount.

However, you will still need to, albeit at your own pace. This is because the insurance companies apply interest rates on your amount, which will keep on increasing. The rates are determined by what kind of policy you have, but it also depends upon how much you have borrowed, and the time taken to pay them back. Taking out a large sum and having them unpaid for longer periods will incur more interest than small amounts that you pay back quickly.

There are four types of interests that your insurance company can charge you:

1. Interest in Advance:

In this type, the policyholder has to pay the interest on that year in advance or when taking out the loan. This is applied when the insurer calculates and infers that the borrowed amount with the interest would exceed the policy coverage amount. This way you can still not pay back the loans but keep your policy from being canceled.

2. Interest in Arrears:

In this type, the policyholder has to pay the interest at the end of the policy year. This interest rate is usually less than the market interest rates and is cheaper.

Fact: Policy year is the one-year period from when you borrowed the money from the policy.

3. Fixed interest rates:

As the name suggests, these interest rates do not change and give the policyholder guarantee that they will remain the same. The policyholder can calculate their loan payment with accuracy in advance.

4. Variable interest rates:

They are not predictable as fixed interest rates and change yearly. They will fluctuate depending on the market interest rates, and the policyholder can only see them when the loan statement is released by the company at the end of the year.

The interest will keep on adding on the borrowed amount and will need to be paid back alongside the original amount, and all the payment needs to be cleared for the loan interest to stop accumulating. Paying the original amount without interest will not clear the loans.

Fact: When you do not pay back the loan, the old interest amount adds to the original amount from which the new interest rate is calculated. This process can be referred to as "Compounding Interest". If ignored, they can substantially increase the debt amount.

Loans Effects on Cash Value Account

In IUL, you can take out loans against your cash value account, and it will not stop or cause an interruption with growing interest inside the policy. The policy's wealth generation will act the same way as though you have not taken the money out.

In this situation, the policyholder can borrow and have some money turned into liquid assets, while the cash value account grows more quickly with the same value.

The cash generation will be quicker, and the borrowed cash can be used for emergencies, other investments, or getting an early retirement for yourself.

Loans and Taxes

According to the IRS, the loans taken out from any life insurance policy, including IUL, are non-taxable. This is true except in the case of loan amounts exceeding the total premium amount paid towards the policy.

During the time the loan is unpaid, if you surrendered or lapsed the policy, then the loan will be considered taxable. Again, the taxable income will only be the amount you have borrowed above your total premium payment.

These tax laws are issued at the federal level, and your local tax laws can additionally apply to your policy loans. To be clear on the subject, it is recommended that you consult with a tax expert upon taking out a loan and verify if any state or local tax laws apply to you.

One of the best parts about these loans is that if you are unable to pay them back, your credit score will be unaffected. The IUL policy cash value account can essentially work as your own personal bank in which you can get loans, tax-free and pay them back.

Is it Worth it to Sell your IUL Policy?

It all depends on the situation. It can be a worthy move if your circumstances call for it. But it can also turn into a disaster if you do not consider all the factors and do not plan it properly.

Before thinking about selling the policy, the policyholder should think about the amount of money they will be left with at the end, after the taxes and charges. Assess whether you want to lose the coverage of your beneficiaries or still want them to have the death benefit help them out in the future.

Even if you are losing money, selling the policy can still be a better option. For example, if the costs of keeping the policy outpace cashing out costs. You may find out that after paying fees, charges, leftover premiums, and penalties, you will actually have less money than before.

To know whether cashing out is going to be a profitable or a money-saving move, one needs to consider many factors and do thorough analyses of their policy.

Factors to consider are:

- How long did you have the policy?
- How much are the surrender charges?
- Are there any extra penalties for cashing out early?
- How much in taxes will you have to pay for cashing out?

After answering these basic questions, you can determine whether you should or should not go along with the decision. It is possible that you are still confused, then you can contact your insurance advisor or broker for their expert opinion. They can provide you with every detail and quick answer that may take you several hours to find out.

How to Sell your IUL Policy

One should not be buying an IUL policy if one thinks that there is a high chance one will not be able to support it in the future. If you are sure that such an event is unlikely, you should still plan it out of caution. Before even buying the policy, assess and familiarize yourself with the cashing-out process. On the off chance that you might need to go through with it, then you do not hesitate or worry as much.

If you deduce that the IUL policy does not serve its purpose anymore, then you should proceed with the cashing-out process.

Selling your policy consists of three steps:

1. **Decide if Selling Out is the Right Decision**

Life insurance policies serve many purposes to different people, such as one wants to save their family from future financial problems, while the other wants to reduce risks in business, etc. One may believe that they cannot live without life insurance, but your mind might change and decide that it is not as important as you thought it would be. Life circumstances change as well, which might make paying for insurance feel useless.

Some people get the policy when their children are young and want to guarantee their future in the case of their untimely death. When they get older, the problem is no longer there, hence is no need for insurance anymore.

Perhaps you may have lost interest in the cash value account because it is not generating enough money anymore, and due to the market's bad performance, the premium costs have risen to levels you did not anticipate.

To determine whether you need the policy or not, compare your current financial needs with the needs you had when you initially bought the IUL policy. Are they the same?

If not, then assess whether your new needs are benefited from having the IUL policy right now. Will it generate more money, or does any loved one need the death benefit? If not, then ask whether it makes sense for you to continue paying for the premiums. If not, then research whether you could get more profit from selling the policy. If the last answer is yes, then proceed to step 2.

2. See if you Qualify for the Settlement

After you have decided your index universal life insurance policy, no longer serves any purpose and has proven to be losing money and generating it, then start to research or ask your broker whether you qualify for the life settlement.

There are some criteria you will need to fulfill to be able to apply for a life settlement. They are:

- Your policy's coverage amount should at least be worth $100,000.
- The policyholder should be 65 years old or older.

There are calculators to help you find out how much money you can get with your policy account. You can even ask any insurance agent to calculate it for you.

3. Accept the best offer you receive

There are different companies that help you sell your life insurance policies and you should be thorough in selecting one. Be sure that you choose not only a stable, trustworthy company but also one that is committed to giving you the best possible deal.

Find a company that will act according to your financial goals. As a senior, it will be difficult for you to fully grasp the market situation and you can easily be swindled and become a victim of fraud. The company should give you leading protection and complete transparency in the buying and selling process.

Reasons for Selling the IUL Policy

There are plenty of reasons why a policyholder would opt to end their insurance and go for a life settlement. Some of the most popular ones are:

- The Policy is no Longer Needed or has Become Unaffordable

Your life changes over the years, and you may have grown out of the need for the policy. Your premiums, at this point, will become a needless hassle or maybe even expensive as time goes on.

In such instances, you have the option to let the policy lapse and get automatically canceled, or surrendered for the cash value. However, getting a life settlement will generate more cash.

- The Time has come for Retirement or you Need to Pay for a Medical Treatment

You may have planned and saved for retirement, but more than often, people underestimate how much it will cost. Inflation has caused the prices to almost double and triple over the years. It is unlikely that it will not happen again in the future. Life settlements can provide the extra money needed for retirement.

Medical expenses are another headache one faces in old age, and they themselves are rising as well. A home health care or long-term health care plan can be bought with life settlement money.

- You need to Increase your Liquid Assets so quick cash can be used during Rainy Days

The money you receive from a life settlement can help you find numerous things, not just retirement or medicine. You can choose to use the money however you want to. You can finally go on dream vacations, get a house renovation or help your children with college debt.

Advantages and Disadvantages of Selling your Policy

If you ever are wondering about cashing out on your plan, then it will be beneficial to take into consideration all the pros and cons first.

Advantages

- A fast way to get a large payment.
- You will not need to pay premiums anymore.
- The money will exceed the amount you may receive from surrendering the account.
- You can spend the money you like on luxury as well.

Disadvantages

- Your family members will not receive a death benefit anymore
- You may have to pay a lot of taxes on the payment
- You may not qualify for many financial assistance services, such as Medicaid

Index universal life insurance policies can be an exceptional tool in making your financial worries go away and help you develop an asset source in the background. They will come in handy in times of need and even in times when you want to reward yourself.

But be careful when withdrawing cash or taking out loans from your account. Understand all of your options and then take the best way to take money out. If you find that IUL is not generating profits and is becoming a liability instead, do not be afraid to surrender or sell the policy.

IUL Fees

There are many charges you have to pay after buying the IUL policy, and there are many hidden fees that may be cut from your cash value account. So, here is a list of the most common fees associated with the policy.

Fixed IUL Charges

- Premium Load

These include all the administration and policy running charges that are cut from your premium payments before entering the cash value account and funding your life insurance. It is represented as a percentage of your premium payment for the year or month.

- Monthly Charges

In this type of policy, the first ten years are subjected to monthly extra charges. This is generally charged for every $1,000 in the death benefit.

Variable IUL Charges

- Mortality Charges

This is a fee charged to the policy before your death. It is a charge to compensate the insurance company for any loss they will suffer at the time of your death.

- Expense Charges

This is an insignificant fee that is charged on the policy. It lasts for the entire policy period.

Summary

- At the time of your death, the IUL policy will transfer the coverage amount of the policy to your beneficiaries. The money saved in your cash value account is not transferable and will be absorbed by the insurance company.
- There are many ways to take money out of your account, which is the main point of having an IUL policy.
- One method is to take money out with withdrawals. The amount of money you can withdraw will be equal to your cost basis. However, some companies can allow you to take more.
- The second method is to take loans, which will be paid back with interest to the insurance company.
- The third method is to surrender the policy. However, you will have to pay surrender charges and your life insurance will be canceled.
- The final method is to sell your IUL insurance policy, which can be more profitable than surrendering.
- There are many reasons why one may need to surrender their account, such as coming across a better deal, premiums getting too high, not needing the account anymore or in emergencies, and wanting quick cash.
- Surrender Value is calculated on the Cost Basis or how much premiums you have paid, along with several other factors.
- You can borrow or loan from your cash value, as high as 90% of the entire account's worth.

- There are many drawbacks to loans, such as your coverage loans will decrease, the interest rates will compound and your policy might get canceled. Taxes are also applied.
- There are advantages of loans as well, such as the interest gains coming into your account will not be interrupted.
- Selling your policy can be worthwhile after carefully assessing if you really need it or not.
- You can sell your policy by deciding if it's a beneficial step, finding out if they are eligible, and finding a deal.
- Many different kinds of fees are applied upon buying the policy. Some of them are mortality charges, monthly charges, and expense charges.

Conclusion

The first thing a person does after graduating is get a job, and they think that life is settled from there. We all are very naïve and clueless at this stage, which might be described as the actual starting point of our life. From then on, we make decisions for ourselves, choose our own future and independently enjoy every second moving forward. It is also the prime time to start thinking about your retirement so that you can spend the last years of your life as comfortable as possible.

Beginning to take action and start exploring retirement options in your 20s is going to ensure your preparedness for the most difficult phase of your life. Being a senior is not an enjoyable task. Your health will be on a decline, and so will your mental prowess. You will not have enough energy to continue to work. The body will start to give in and you no longer will have the luxury of working overtime anymore.

At this point, you will need an income source. A self-sustaining, money-making tool that will find your retirement even after you have retired. A great way to start planning on procuring as a good deal of money-making tools is to consider purchasing an IUL investment/insurance policy.

You could be a family man caring for your young kids, but their lives are only as good as you can make them be. What would happen if you were to suddenly get caught in an accident? What if you develop some sort of medical ailment that can take you away from them? These thoughts may have you waking up at night, especially if you are a single parent with all the responsibilities on your shoulders. In these situations, you cannot afford to slack off and remain an idol of these pressing worries. You have to think about their future and act quickly for them as well.

If you are someone with these anxieties, then life insurance policies must have come across in discussions and Google search bars more often than not. Life insurance is a great way to secure your family's financial goals, even after you die. IUL investment/insurance policies will provide your family with a deserving coverage amount, but that is not all that it can do. With an IUL account, you can save up for your own retirement and rack up extra cash by having your money be, essentially, invested in the stock market. The money you will pay the insurance companies will not only go towards funding the life insurance policy for your family but also getting more shares on a popular index of the stock market for you as well.

There are many other life insurance policies out there, and perhaps other types may suit you better than IUL, especially if you are not as interested in having a part of your investment tied to your life insurance policy. However, to truly understand whether they are for you, first, you need to understand the different policies, your own financial needs, and goals. Only after careful analysis, an individual can truly deduce which policy is right for them.

IUL policies have a cash value account in which a part of your money is stored and tied to the index to keep growing up with the good performance of the aforementioned index. The best part is, unlike in direct investing, there is no risk of losing money. Many more benefits make this life insurance policy a great choice for people wanting life insurance and also a retirement fund.

Perhaps index universal life insurance policies are not for you, but how will you know for sure if you never learned about them in the first place? This book does not just describe the details of this policy, but also explores the different aspects of other types of life insurance policies so you know the pros and cons of other financial services and make informed decisions. You can advise your friends and family about life insurance easily, regardless of their financial status and limitations.

Now that you have been informed about the terms and inner workings of life insurance policies, especially IUL, you can begin your process of opening up your account and start preparing for the best retirement of your life. Having a good retirement plan does not only affect you but also affects the people that are close to you. Certainly, by not being smart and not taking action early, one can become a burden on their family members. Children leave their goals and ambitions behind and take on the responsibilities of providing and caring for their parents. Taking action for retirement early on means that you care about your family members as well.

The best time to start planning is as soon as possible, no matter what your age might be. You could be in your 20s or 30s, or maybe you are entering your 50s. No one can reverse time, but as long as you start to take calculated steps toward financial independence, you will feel the benefits of it. Some will feel fewer benefits, some more, but none will be disappointed because ultimately it will give a helping hand during the most vulnerable time of your life.

The importance of exploring new opportunities, especially in finance, is greatly underestimated. There are various methods by which people are creating, maintaining, and growing their wealth, and many of us are ignorant and unaware of them, simply thinking that 9 to 5 is the only way to live. You can explore these options and also be a flourishing, contributing member of society. By taking opportunity after opportunity, one or two are sure to land, and they will make all the difference.

When we are stuck in a mundane job, life loses its color and meaning, and we yearn for retirement. – a grim reality gave the fact that we will be closer to the end of our life. By planning, learning, and taking action, one can reach retirement goals early on, when they are healthy and energized. By taking smart financial steps, you can achieve dreams which you once thought were unachievable. You can buy that big house or car, go on tours and vacations, finally try that new business idea or have the ability to pay for your child's college. The result of proper financial planning is endless.

Remember to prioritize a healthy body and mind above anything else, and get out of the notion of constantly doing part time and overtime. Start to save and invest more often. Focus on education, being informed, and letting the money make more money for you. It is far better than grinding your body with every cent. You will not have the luxury to do so in your old age anyway, so why not opt for a more long-term solution?

IUL and other financial services are here to help the public achieve their financial goals, however, it is up to you to decide which ones will help you the most.

References

A Brief History of Universal Life. (n.d.). https://www.soa.org/globalassets/assets/library/monographs/50th-anniversary/product-development-section/1999/january/m-as99-3-06.pdf

Access Denied. (n.d.). https://www.allstate.com/resources/life-insurance/variable-universal-life-insurance

B. (2022a, August 2). *IUL vs. Roth IRA: Which One is Better for Your Retirement Savings?* BravoPolicy. https://bravopolicy.com/life-insurance/iul-vs-roth-ira/

Beal Financial Group - IUL vs 401 (K). (n.d.). https://www.bealfinancialgroup.com/iul-vs-401-k

Bond, C. (2022, August 5). *When And Why To Surrender A Life Insurance Policy.* Forbes Advisor. https://www.forbes.com/advisor/life-insurance/surrender-life-insurance-policy/

Can I Withdraw Money From My Universal Life Insurance Policy? (2020, September 2). Life Ant. https://www.lifeant.com/faq/can-i-withdraw-money-from-my-universal-life-insurance-policy/

Cooper, S. (2022, November 23). *A Look at IUL Fees, Costs, & Illustration Manipulation.* FIG Marketing. https://www.figmarketing.com/blog/a-look-at-iul-fees-costs-and-illustration-manipulation/

Croll, M. (2022, November 2). *What is Universal Life Insurance? Pros and Cons*. ValuePenguin. https://www.valuepenguin.com/life-insurance/universal-life-insurance

D. (n.d.). *Universal Life Insurance, Indexed Universal Life, Variable Life Insurance*. https://www.mutualofomaha.com/life-insurance/universal-life-insurance

Episode #4: The Costs Associated with an Indexed Universal Life Policy. (n.d.). https://www.lifepro.com/Blog/PostId/1792/the-costs-associated-with-an-indexed-universal-life-policy

Episode #31: What Type of Return Can I Expect from My IUL Policy? (n.d.). https://www.lifepro.com/Blog/PostId/1827/what-type-of-return-can-i-expect-from-my-iul-policy

Forbidden | Error | SmartAsset.com. (n.d.). https://smartasset.com/retirement/indexed-universal-life-insurance-iul

George, D. (2023, February 22). *Indexed Universal Life (IUL) Insurance: What It Is and Whether It's for You*. The Motley Fool. https://www.fool.com/the-ascent/insurance/life/indexed-universal-life-insurance-iul/

H. (2022b, June 14). *Historical Market Movements and IUL*. Banking Truths. https://bankingtruths.com/videos/market-history-and-iul/

How Variable Universal Life Insurance Works | Thrivent. (2023, January 23). Thrivent.com. https://www.thrivent.com/insights/life-insurance/how-variable-universal-life-insurance-works

Huffman, E. (2022, June 24). *Best Variable Life Insurance for February 2023* •. Benzinga. https://www.benzinga.com/money/best-variable-life-insurance

Index Universal Life Insurance. (n.d.). Transamerica. https://www.transamerica.com/insurance/index-universal-life-insurance

Indexed Universal Life Insurance Buying Guide | Guardian. (n.d.). https://www.guardianlife.com/life-insurance/indexed-universal

Indexed Universal Life Insurance (IUL) Meaning and Pros and Cons. (2022, November 4). Investopedia. https://www.investopedia.com/articles/personal-finance/012416/pros-and-cons-indexed-universal-life-insurance.asp

Indexed Universal Life (IUL) Explained. (n.d.). Ogletree Financial. https://insurancequotes2day.com/indexed-universal-life-iul-explained/

Iversen, J. (2022, September 20). *How to use Indexed Universal Life [IUL] Insurance - WealthFit.* https://wealthfit.com. https://wealthfit.com/articles/iul-indexed-universal-life-insurance/

Kamel, G. (2023, February 3). *Indexed Universal Life Insurance (IUL), Explained.* Ramsey Solutions. https://www.ramseysolutions.com/insurance/indexed-universal-life-insurance

Kilroy, A. (2022, April 11). *Universal Life Insurance Explained.* Forbes Advisor. https://www.forbes.com/advisor/life-insurance/universal-life-insurance/

Leefeldt, E. (2022, November 11). *Sounding The Alarm On Indexed Universal Life Insurance (IUL).* Forbes Advisor. https://www.forbes.com/advisor/life-insurance/indexed-universal-life-insurance-problems/

Lighthouse Life Solutions, LLC. (2022, December 12). *How to Sell a Universal Life Insurance Policy for Cash.* Lighthouse Life. https://www.lighthouselife.com/blog/how-to-sell-a-universal-life-insurance-policy-for-cash/

Marder, A., & Rose, G. (2023, January 12). *What is Universal Life Insurance? Pros, Cons and Cost.* NerdWallet. https://www.nerdwallet.com/article/insurance/universal-life-insurance

Newth, M. (2022, June 14). *IUL's Fees Examined and Explained.* Banking Truths. https://bankingtruths.com/videos/iul-charges/

Plummer, S. (2022, July 27). *How To Cash Out A Life Insurance Policy Before Death? (2023).* The Annuity Expert. https://www.annuityexpertadvice.com/cash-out-life-insurance-policy-before-death/

Policygenius. (n.d.). https://www.policygenius.com/life-insurance/how-to-cancel-your-life-insurance-policy/

Pros and Cons of Indexed Universal Life Insurance. (2022, November 22). Investopedia. https://www.investopedia.com/articles/personal-finance/070215/pros-cons-indexed-universal-life-insurance.asp

Registered Indexed Universal Life. (n.d.). https://us.milliman.com/-/media/milliman/pdfs/articles/registered-indexed-universal-life-concept-paper.ashx

Schneider, J. (2023, February 14). *Is IUL a Scam? Yes.* Personal Finance Club. https://www.personalfinanceclub.com/is-iul-a-scam-yes/

Scott, S. (2022, September 23). *What You Need to Know About Universal Life Insurance Pros and Cons*. Healthmarkets Agents/Content/Plans. https://www.healthmarkets.com/resources/life-insurance/look-universal-life-insurance-pros-cons/

Six Key Steps to Setting up an IUL the Better Money Method Way | The Better Money Method. (2018, March 5). https://www.bettermoneymethod.com/six-key-steps-creating-iul-policy-works/

Top 10 Best Indexed Universal Life (IUL) Insurance Companies. (2023, January 26). https://www.insuranceandestates.com/indexed-universal-life-iul-insurance/

Van Haaften, E. (2023, February 9). *Life Insurance Policy Loans*. Affordable Life USA. https://affordablelifeusa.com/life-insurance-policy-loans/

Variable Life Insurance. (2022, December 13). Investopedia. https://www.investopedia.com/ask/answers/08/variable-life-insurance.asp

Variable Universal Life (VUL) Insurance: What It Is, How It Works. (2022, June 14). Investopedia. https://www.investopedia.com/terms/v/variableuniversallife.asp

What Are Surrender Charges? Definition, How They Work and Example. (2022, July 18). Investopedia. https://www.investopedia.com/terms/s/surrendercharge.asp

What Is Indexed Universal Life Insurance (IUL)? (2023, February 22). Investopedia. https://www.investopedia.com/articles/insurance/09/indexed-universal-life-insurance.asp

What Is Universal Life Insurance? (n.d.). https://www.davidraefp.com/What-Is-Universal-Life-Insurance.c43.htm

Made in the USA
Monee, IL
04 November 2026

67385787R00095